Ad Iesum per Mariam—to Jesus through Mary—is the high road of Christian faith and devotion and has been from the start. In *Keeping Mary Close*, Mike Aquilina and Fr. Gruber provide a scholarly and engaging overview of this fascinating history for the instruction and edification of today's reader. This is a book to read, cherish for your own enrichment, and share with family and friends.

—Russell Shaw, author, *American Church*

Keeping Mary Close is one of the very rare Marian titles that will help the reader to appreciate both the why and the how of our devotion to the Blessed Mother. Mike Aquilina and Fr. Gruber take us on a journey into theology, history, devotion, and prayer that ends with a deeper understanding of Mary. This is a perfect book for anyone who wants to understand the place of the Mother of God in the life of the Church and to defend her rightful place in the lives of all Christians.

—Matthew Bunson, author, *Pope Francis*

I've read a lot of books about Mary. This is one of the best. Aquilina and Gruber provide a beautifully unique perspective of Our Lady through the lens of early Church history. It's a fascinating journey through the mind of the Church into the heart of its Mother.

—Matthew Leonard, executive director,
St. Paul Center for Biblical Theology

Mike Aquilina and Fr. Fredrick Gruber have authored a magnificent little book on Mary. Not only do they give us a splendid and lucid account of the theological development concerning Mary as the Mother of Jesus, particularly through the eyes of the Fathers of the Church, but they also beautifully show how this theological understanding of Mary nurtured a deep love and devotion to Mary through the ages. They illuminate the truth that to know and love Mary, the Mother of God, is to know and love Jesus, the Father's Son.

—Thomas G. Weinandy, O.F.M., CAP., member of the
Vatican's International Theological Commission

Mike Aquilina steered me to the works of Fr. Luigi Gambari years ago, which enriched my love for Mary as participant in the Mystery of the Incarnation even more than before. Fr. Fredrick Gruber is a leading expert in Coptic Christianity, which is also dear to my heart due to its monastic heart, and the heart of the Holy Family in Egypt. In this short work they have compressed into one short volume a most artful presentation of vast ancient ages of Christianity. If you love Jesus, and are in awe of the Incarnation of the Logos, this book will stir your heart to greater love of and devotion to Mary, the Mother of Jesus. Read it. Pray it. And be drawn into the Mystery of God Incarnate and the heart of the Church!

—John Michael Talbot, author,
The Master Musician: Meditations on Jesus

KEEPING MARY CLOSE

*Devotion to Our Lady
through the Ages*

MIKE AQUILINA
and
FR. FREDERICK W. GRUBER

servant

AN IMPRINT OF
FRANCISCAN MEDIA
Cincinnati, Ohio

Cover and book design by Mark Sullivan
Cover image © Godong/UIG/Bridgeman Images

LIBRARY OF CONGRESS CATALOGING-IN-PUBLICATION DATA
Aquilina, Mike.
Keeping Mary close : devotion to Our Lady through the ages / Mike Aquilina and Fr. Frederick W. Gruber.
pages cm
Includes bibliographical references and index.
ISBN 978-1-61636-874-6 (alk. paper)
1. Mary, Blessed Virgin, Saint—Devotion to—History. 2. Church history—Primitive and early church, ca. 30-600. I. Title.
BT645.A68 2015
232.9109—dc23
2015027621

ISBN 978-1-61636-874-6

Published by Servant, an imprint of Franciscan Media
28 W. Liberty St.
Cincinnati, OH 45202
www.FranciscanMedia.org

Printed in the United States of America.
Printed on acid-free paper.
15 16 17 18 19 5 4 3 2 1

To our mothers,
who showed us the way to Jesus
through Mary.

"Imitate her, holy mothers, who in affection to her only dearly
beloved Son set forth so great an example of maternal virtue."
— St. Ambrose of Milan[1]

⚛ CONTENTS

YOU HOLD IN YOUR HANDS A GREAT TREASURE: A WINDOW INTO the world of early Christian devotion. And when you look through that window, what you will see is a deep and enduring love and appreciation for Mary, the mother of Jesus.

Mary was the first Christian, the first to say yes to Jesus, when the angel presented her with the divine plan of the Incarnation (see Luke 1:26–38). Or to put it in popular evangelical terms, she was the first person ever to accept Jesus as her Savior.

In this way, and in many others, Mary is our prototype—the first one like us who welcomed Jesus into her life and walked the path of discipleship. Just as she received Christ into her body, in her womb, so we also receive Christ into our bodies when we take his Body and Blood in the Holy Eucharist.

Mary's importance for the Church, and for history, cannot be overestimated. She is as important as Jesus's inner circle of disciples: Peter, James, and John. She is as important as Paul. Graffiti in the Roman catacombs record the prayers of second- and third-century Christians—prayers asking for the intercession of Peter, Paul, and Mary. When the *chi-rho* monogram of Christ became a popular Christian symbol in the fourth century, it was often embellished to include the initials of Peter and Mary. And Mary is the only one of Jesus's followers to be mentioned in the creeds.

Mary is the Ark of the New Covenant. Just as the ark of the original covenant held the Word of God in the Ten Commandments, the womb of Mary held the divine Word of God, united to our human nature and incarnate. This is just one of the images the Church fathers used to talk about Mary. In this book, Mike Aquilina and Fr. Gruber will introduce you to many of those early Christian teachers as well as the beautiful and diverse ways they taught about—and practiced—devotion to Mary.

For me personally, as a Catholic Christian of the late twentieth and early twenty-first centuries—and as a historian of the early Christian centuries—Mary is a mother, a pioneer, a prayer partner, an intercessor, and especially the patroness of the culture of life that I hope will increase in our country and in the world. I see Mary as one of Jesus's first disciples, but I also see her as Jesus's first teacher. After all, who but Mary could have told Jesus about his own miraculous birth? She was the first to be aware of Jesus's identity. The twelve-year-old Jesus's words to her, "How is it that you sought me? Did you not know that I must be in my Father's house?" (Luke 2:49), imply that they both knew something the rest of the world would learn later.

So Mary matters. She matters so much, in fact, that the one to whom Jesus entrusted her would later write of her in glorious terms, as "a woman clothed with the sun, with the moon under her feet, and on her head a crown of twelve stars" (Revelation 12:1). After describing the birth of Jesus and Herod's attempt to have him killed (depicted as an act of the dragon, Satan), and then the Holy Family's flight into Egypt, John goes on say that "the dragon was angry with the woman, and went off to make war on *the rest of her offspring, on those who keep the command-ments and bear testimony to Jesus*" (Revelation 12:17, emphasis added). This is a reference to the persecution of the Church, but my point is that "the rest of [Mary's] offspring" is the Church. We are her other children. She is our mother, just as Jesus said to John, "Behold, your mother!" (John 19:26–27).

Everything we believe about Mary tells us something about her Son. This is most evident in the ancient title *Mother of God*, for it affirms the divinity of Christ. Mary's role in the Church is in many ways defined by her own words in John 2:5, when she pointed to Jesus and said to the waiters, "Do whatever he tells you." This is still her message to us. And even more than that, she prays for us as we do our best to follow her advice.

This is an important book because it puts us in touch with the great "cloud of witnesses" (Hebrews 12:1), our ancestors in the faith, who lived in a time much closer to that of Jesus and the apostles than our own. This book will allow you to hear from the Fathers in their own words how much Mary meant to them, how much Mary meant to their faith, and how they met Mary in prayer.

As I write this, Easter is approaching, but before Easter comes Good Friday—the day on which Mary's own soul was pierced (see Luke 2:35), when her Son was crucified. This year (2015), there is little more than a week between the Feast of the Annunciation of the Blessed Virgin Mary (March 25) and Good Friday—between the celebration of the Incarnation on one hand and the passion of our Lord on the other. What a poignant juxtaposition. It was for this that he came into the world, and it was through her that he came into the world. It is no wonder, then, that she should be called blessed throughout all ages (see Luke 1:48).

———

Dr. Papandrea is associate professor of Church history at Garrett-Evangelical Theological Seminary. He is the author of many books on the early Church and on the spiritual life.

❈ ACKNOWLEDGMENTS

WE ARE GRATEFUL TO ALL THE GOOD TEACHERS AND EXEMPLARS we've known in our years of studying the Fathers. As we prepared this book, three scholars in particular were very helpful.

The anthropologist Mark Gruber, expert in the field of Coptic Christianity, answered many questions for us (at all hours of the day and night) and produced relevant sources instantly. Adrian Murdoch—fellow of the British Royal Historical Society—helped us evaluate the Marian material of Julian the Apostate (about whom he wrote the definitive biography). And we were pleased to have the assistance of the eminent patrologist James Papandrea whenever we called upon him.

We honor the memory of Fr. Luigi Gambero, whose books have enriched both of us—and whose classroom teaching formed one of us.

Kevin Knight (NewAdvent.org) and Roger Pearse (Tertullian. org) generously allowed us to use and adapt their e-texts for this book. May God bless them abundantly. Most of the texts are from the nineteenth-century translations published in two series: *The Ante-Nicene Fathers* and *The Nicene and Post-Nicene Fathers*.[1] Other rare translations are scattered around Project Gutenberg and on Roger Pearse's site. We have taken the liberty of modernizing the English to make it more accessible to today's readers.

We also thank the editors of the multivolume *Ancient Christian Commentary on Scripture*, published by InterVarsity Press (2001). It is a remarkable resource. Would that it were on the shelves of every student and teacher of ancient history—and every preacher in Christ's Church.

Finally, we must thank St. Joseph, whose assistance was constant throughout this project. We knew he would help us make something good for his spouse, our mother.

CHAPTER ONE

FROM JERUSALEM TO EPHESUS ⚎

> Then they returned to Jerusalem.... And when they had
> entered, they went up to the upper room, where they were
> staying, Peter and John and James and Andrew, Philip
> and Thomas, Bartholomew and Matthew, James the son
> of Alphaeus and Simon the Zealot and Judas the son of
> James. All these with one accord devoted themselves to
> prayer, together with the women and Mary the mother of
> Jesus, and with his brothers. (Acts 1:12–14)

THAT IS HOW THE ORIGINAL CHURCH DESCRIBED ITSELF. THE
words come from a meticulous historian of the first generation, St.
Luke the evangelist, who testified that he had interviewed eyewitnesses (see Luke 1:1–4).

In the days after Jesus's ascension, the disciples awaited the gift
the Lord had promised as the seal of their salvation. In the Upper
Room, they waited to be filled with the Holy Spirit. They gathered
"together with...Mary the mother of Jesus."

That was the primitive Church on its own terms. The Blessed
Virgin Mary was in its midst. She was a disciple among disciples,
and yet her place and her role were unique. In the Acts passage
above, she is the only woman to be mentioned by name; in fact,
she is the only non-apostle to be identified. And as the last named,
she holds a place of prominence.

She is a quiet presence, but constant and crucial. She changes the composition of the picture. Suddenly the Upper Room is more than a waiting room in an all-male seminary. There is a feminine presence identified as *mother*. The gathering is a family, and the room becomes a home.

And that is how the Church viewed itself throughout its early life. Mary remained a presence, often acknowledged, clearly loved and honored, and necessary for the coherence of the gospel's proclamation.

This book is about devotion to Mary in that period, the so-called patristic era—the time most people mean when they speak of the "early Church." The period begins with Christianity's first generation. Some of these Fathers—Clement, Ignatius, and Polycarp—received the faith directly from the apostles.

Through most of the period that concerns us, the practice of the faith was illegal, and sometimes it was a capital crime. Periods of intense persecution, however, were also times of intense devotion. Something worth dying for was also worth protecting, preserving, and passing on. Because our ancestors in the Church took risks to preserve so many prayers, sermons, and letters, we can—with some degree of confidence—write a book about the Marian devotion of those ancestors.

Signs of Devotion

The beginning of the patristic era is fairly clear, but historians differ on the date when it ended. Many say it closed with the death of St. John of Damascus in A.D. 749, though some extend it to the close of the first millennium (A.D. 1000) and others draw the line at the death of St. Bernard of Clairvaux (1153). Both John and Bernard were passionate in their love for the Blessed

Virgin—having a remarkable influence on all future Marian reflection in the East and West respectively—and it is tempting to include them in our study. But we've decided that the scope of this book should be much smaller.

We'll concentrate instead on the period from roughly A.D. 30 to A.D. 431. The first date corresponds (again, roughly) to the scene we evoked at the beginning of this chapter, the scene in the Upper Room. The latter date corresponds to the great Council of Ephesus. It was at Ephesus that the bishops of the world summarized, synthesized, and dogmatically proclaimed the key Marian teachings of the centuries before. This was the crowning moment of the early Church's Marian devotion. Ephesus, then, is a helpful vantage point from which we can look back and see the very beginning.

Focusing on the first four centuries will also allow us to correct some common misconceptions about the early Church. In the last couple centuries, it has been fashionable for scholars in the English-speaking world to minimize or dismiss the ancient Church's Marian devotion. This tendency first arose in the years after the Reformation, when Protestant scholars sought to justify their churches' rupture with Catholic traditions regarding Mary. Over time, this anti-Mariology became reflexive—a "Mary allergy," so to speak—and even some Catholics adopted it in order to advance in their professions.

The contemporary historian Stephen Shoemaker writes of an "anti-Catholic prejudice" and "bias" in his field, a "prejudice of early Christian studies against attributing much significance to the veneration of Mary before the council of Ephesus." "There is," he said, "a palpable tendency in much scholarship to minimize the strong devotion to Mary evident in the ancient church."[1] The tendency is to reduce devotion to cult—the official public worship of the Church—and then, further, to interpret *cult* even more narrowly as direct invocation. So the only true instance of Marian devotion, for such scholars, would be a prayer addressed directly to Mary, asking for her intercession.

Devotion, however, involves much more than that. There is ample evidence of devotion to Saints Peter and Paul in the same period. We know this from intercessory prayers, yes, but also from artwork, from shrines dedicated to the apostles, from graffiti scratched on plaster walls, from feast days celebrated far and wide, and from books that describe their heroic deeds and teachings.

As in the Acts of the Apostles, so in those first centuries: Mary's is a quiet presence in the Church, but it is no less real and persistent than those of Peter and Paul. It is, in fact, more important in the history of Christian doctrine.

In considering the role of Mary in the Church, we will look to the words of the ancients and also to the recent findings of archeology. From the first century to the fifth, we find hymns about Mary, books about her, paintings of her, as well as sculptures and graffiti praising her. Fabrics and jewelry, wall decorations and oil lamps bear witness to the Church's devotion to Mary. And throughout the early life of the Church, we find great men fiercely defending her.

We find devotion. It is not as diffuse as the devotion to Saints Peter and Paul but more concentrated and intense. It is, moreover, distinct from any other Christian devotion. It is altogether different from devotion to the Persons of the Blessed Trinity, yet it is elevated above the devotion given to other saints and martyrs. Mary's place in the early Church, like her place in the Scriptures, is uniquely "blessed."

After centuries of explaining such evidence away, academic history has begun to recognize this. As universities turn increasingly secular, more historians—wary of both Protestant and Catholic polemics—have been willing to reexamine the evidence from the early Christian centuries. This has been good for the Catholic cause and especially for the study of the Blessed Virgin Mary. This book takes full advantage of that new wave of research.

Developing Doctrine and Devotion

We do not, of course, possess as many documents and artifacts from this period as we would like to have. Still, those that we do have amount to thousands of pages, and it is interesting to note how many of the early documents mention Mary. Sometimes the mention is as brief, but also as significant, as St. Luke's glance in the Acts of the Apostles. In other instances, Mary is the center of attention. She is treated consistently with tenderness, love, and admiration—with devotion.

In other words, it seems that the early Christians approached Mary as Catholics do today. This does not mean they prayed with rosary beads—they did not. This does not mean they wore the brown scapular of Our Lady of Mount Carmel—they did not. This does not mean they prayed novenas to Our Lady of Perpetual Help—they did not. Nor did they join parish sodalities, or sponsor May Crownings, or pray the *Memorare* and *Salve Regina*. The ancients did few of the things most closely associated with modern Marian devotion. Yet all of our modern and medieval practices *developed* from the doctrines and practices of the

Church of the Fathers. They correspond to the model of devotion established by our ancestors.

Such development—in both doctrine and devotion—is faithful to the pattern set by the ancient Fathers. St. Basil the Great wrote in the fourth century:

> The same doctrine has been developed through progress, and what now is mine has not taken the place of what existed in the beginning....
>
> Through progress we observe a certain amplification of what we say, which is not a change from worse to better, but is a completing of that which was lacking, according to the increment of our knowledge.[2]

Development, as the Fathers understood it, is not innovation; it introduces nothing new to the faith that the Church has received from Jesus through the apostles. Nor is it an evolution; it does not cause the faith to morph into something different from what it has been since the beginning. Development is, rather, an elaboration—a deepening of understanding. Development makes explicit what is implicit in the Scriptures.

The classic example of doctrinal development is the Church's teaching on the Godhead. The word *Trinity* appears nowhere in Scripture. In fact, it appears nowhere at all (in its Greek or Latin forms) until rather late in the second century. It is implicit, of course, in the New Testament. In the last verses of St. Matthew's Gospel, Jesus told his disciples to baptize "in the name of the Father and of the Son and of the Holy Spirit" (Matthew 28:19)—a singular "name" of three distinct Persons. St. Paul blessed his congregations in this name: "The grace of the Lord Jesus Christ and the love of God and the fellowship of the Holy

Spirit be with you all" (2 Corinthians 13:14).

It fell to future generations to elaborate on these blessings in their proclamations and rites of worship. It fell to the Fathers to draw out the implications of the apostolic teaching, applying it to new historical circumstances and vastly different cultures. Development was inevitable, because it is a natural part of life—and the Church is a living body. Already in the second century, Tertullian highlighted the role of the Holy Spirit in development:

> The reason why the Lord sent the Paraclete was, that, since human mediocrity was unable to take in all things at once, discipline should, little by little, be directed, and ordained, and carried on to perfection, by that Vicar of the Lord, the Holy Spirit.... Nothing is without stages of growth: all things await their season.[3]

St. Irenaeus of Lyons, also writing in the second century, spoke of development as evidence of the Church's capacity for perpetual renewal:

> The preaching of the Church is everywhere consistent, and continues in an even course, and receives testimony from the prophets, the apostles, and all the disciples.... Since it has been received from the Church, we guard this faith. Constantly its youth is renewed by the Spirit of God, as if it were some precious deposit in an excellent vessel; and it causes the vessel containing it also to renew its youth....[4]

Occasions of Instruction

Both doctrine and devotion developed most richly in times when the Church was threatened most seriously by heresy. To the challenge of error, the faithful responded with new forms of prayer adapted from ancient traditions. To the attacks of the heretics, the bishops and theologians responded with an ever-closer reading of Scripture. St. Augustine described this process:

> The fevered restlessness of heretics stirs questions about many articles of the Catholic faith. But the need to defend them forces us to investigate them more accurately, understand them more clearly, and proclaim them more earnestly. So the question raised by an adversary becomes the occasion of instruction.[5]

Each critical dispute, then, led to a clearer statement of the ancient faith. What was formerly implicit in the Bible and in Christian worship became gradually explicit in doctrine.

Most of the ancient heresies posed threats to the apostolic teaching about Jesus Christ—about his Person, his human and divine natures, and his relationship to God the Father and the Holy Spirit. It was in responding to errors about Jesus that the Fathers were led to speak more clearly about Mary. Thus, our great witnesses in this book are those Fathers who most courageously defended the orthodox doctrine of Jesus Christ.

We will hear from St. Ignatius as he battled the second-century Docetist heresy, Athanasius as he fought against Arianism, and Cyril as he battled the errors of Nestorius. These Fathers knew that a proper understanding of Jesus required a proper understanding of his mother. Marian devotion was, for them, a sign of healthy devotion to Jesus—a sign of true faith.

St. Cyril of Alexandria fought for a proper doctrine of Jesus Christ, but his struggle began because the new bishop in the empire's capital was discouraging traditional Marian prayers. "For you must surely know," Cyril said, "that almost all our fight for the faith arose in connection with our insistence that the holy virgin is the Mother of God."[6]

The Fathers knew that errors about Mary necessarily implied errors about her Son—errors, therefore, that they could not abide in good conscience. All things work together for the good of those who love God (see Romans 8:28). Where heresy abounded, truth abounded more (Romans 5:20). Even offenses against Christ became occasions of grace as the Fathers responded, and ordinary Christians grew in their understanding and piety—as the faith underwent development in doctrine and devotion.

Full of Grace

Because the Fathers prevailed, those early Christian congregations enjoyed a healthy devotion to the Mother of God. They did not hesitate to address her as the angel Gabriel did: "Hail, full of grace! The Lord is with you!" Those phrases are embedded in the early Egyptian Eucharistic prayer, the Liturgy of St. Mark.[7]

And yes, the early Christians invoked the intercession of the Mother of God. They did not hesitate to "fly to her patronage," as we see in one prayer from third-century Egypt.[8] In the mid-fourth century, St. Gregory of Nazianzus told the story of St. Justina of Antioch, a consecrated virgin who was in danger of being raped. She begged the help of the Virgin Mary and won not only the rescue she wanted but also the conversion of her attacker.[9]

It is most interesting that, as Gregory told the story, he mentioned Mary's favor in passing. He didn't qualify, didn't clarify, and didn't explain it. He assumed that Marian devotion was already part of life for every Christian in his congregation; it needed no footnotes.

The *Sibylline Oracles*, which are very ancient but notoriously hard to date, credit Mary's intercession for still greater mercies. Almighty God, they tell us, "gave seven ages of repentance to erring humanity, thanks to the holy Virgin."[10]

Marian intercession was simply part of the Christian package. It belonged to Scripture and tradition, to the deposit of faith. It brought people to Jesus Christ. It brought Christ's tender mercy to his people.

How important was the Blessed Virgin to the faith of the early Church? She was essential. Writing in the middle of the third century, Origen of Alexandria evoked the scene at the cross, as the Beloved Disciple stood with Mary, and Jesus said to the disciple, "Behold, your mother," and said to his mother, "Woman, behold your son" (John 19:26–28). Origen commented that no one could understand the gospel—no one could be Jesus's "beloved disciple"—"unless he has reclined upon the breast of Jesus and received from Jesus Mary to be his mother, too."[11]

St. Ambrose of Milan took that observation and made it a summons. He said: "Let Christ say to you from the yoke of the cross, 'Behold, your mother.'... Then you will begin to be a son of the Church."[12]

When the Fathers preached about Mary, they preached in a memorable way. They called her Spouse of Joseph, Mother of Christ, Mother of Jesus, Mother of God, Mother of the Church, Mother of All Living, Ever Virgin, Virgin Mother, and New Eve. All of those titles emerged from the piety of the ancient Church. Each bears theological freight, and each has lasting consequences for Christian life and devotion.

All for Jesus

The era of classic Marian devotion began, as we have said, in a quiet way, and it proceeded quietly for centuries. But if there was one unquiet moment in the early Church's Marian devotion, it was at the very end of the era, at the conclusion of the Council of Ephesus. If it had taken place in May, we might consider it the great "May Crowning" of the patristic era, for there the Fathers crowned the doctrine of their predecessors.

Leading the council as president was St. Cyril of Alexandria, a man so devoted to his sainted forebears that he earned the nickname "Seal of the Fathers." Cyril made sure that every argument he made was shored up with a chain of citations from the early Fathers.

In the sweltering heat of the summer of 431, the council met to decide whether the title "Mother of God" (in Greek, *Theotokos*) should be permitted. For the final session, the bishops gathered behind closed doors in the city's Church of St. Mary. And while the bishops deliberated inside, a crowd gathered outside. Not long into daylight, the whole population of Ephesus had arrived, and there they stayed, praying in the heat throughout the day, awaiting word of the bishops' decision. When the bishops emerged after dusk, they announced their decision in favor of the tradition—in favor of the long-held custom of addressing Mary as Mother of God.

The crowd erupted with joy and began to sing hymns to the Virgin (the ancient equivalents, no doubt, of today's favorites, "Immaculate Mary" and "Hail, Holy Queen"). The men moved out from the church in torchlight procession, and the women arrived with incense to accompany the bishops on the way back to their lodgings. It was one of the most beautifully boisterous celebrations recorded from the early Christian centuries. And it was all for Jesus, through Mary.

We should strive to hear their shouts. The passionate Marian devotion of Christians in the first centuries can and should inspire us in the twenty-first. That it may be so, and that this book may amplify those ancient voices, is the ardent prayer of the authors.

CHAPTER TWO

MARY IN THE BIBLE ⊞

THE FATHERS, IF ASKED, WOULD SURELY SAY THAT THE SOURCES of Marian devotion are the events recorded in the biblical texts. Almost everything we know about Mary comes from the pages of the New Testament, especially the Gospels.

Mary's role in the drama of Jesus's life is unique and pivotal. It is something less than starring but more than supporting. The only characters comparable in the Gospels, in terms of importance, are John the Baptist and Peter. Unlike the apostles, however, Mary is never shown to fail in virtue. Unlike even John the Baptist, she always seems to move forward with a clear sense of God's purpose.

She is the only character who remained with Jesus from his first earthly days to the very end. In the beginning of the narrative, she has many spoken parts. As Jesus begins his public ministry, she trails off into silence and simple presence. The Fathers saw significance in her words but also in her diminishment and silence.

In this chapter we will briefly review the biblical passages the Fathers used most often in their Marian preaching, teaching, and other devotion. (Many of these passages were also favorite subjects of early Christian sculptors and painters.) We will refer to the Fathers' reflections only in passing, as they will be discussed at greater length in other chapters.

Eyewitness Report

St. Luke contributes the most to the New Testament, even more than St. Paul or St. John, and St. Luke gives Mary the most extensive coverage. From as early as the second century, we have the testimony of Tertullian that "Luke's form of the Gospel men usually ascribe to Paul."[1] As Luke traveled and evangelized alongside Paul, it seems that he recorded the apostle's teachings. Hence it is significant that St. Luke gives Mary the most extensive coverage.

The author of the third Gospel and the Acts of the Apostles, Luke is—of the four evangelists—the one who most consciously observes the methods of ancient historians. At the start of his Gospel, he says that his purpose is to "compile a narrative of the things which have been accomplished among us, just as they were delivered to us by those who from the beginning were eyewitnesses" (Luke 1:1–2). "Eyewitness" testimony is important to Luke, and he was himself an eyewitness to some of the events recorded in the Acts of the Apostles.

Mary is the only possible eyewitness to the annunciation and the only likely firsthand source for Luke's account of the visitation and nativity. It seems that Zechariah and Elizabeth were very old at the time of the events, and St. Joseph apparently had died by the beginning of Jesus's ministry. Luke, moreover, does not hesitate to tell his readers what Mary "considered in her mind" (Luke 1:29) or "kept" and pondered "in her heart" (Luke 2:19, 51). The only other person whose thoughts he discloses is Jesus (see 6:8; 9:47). In Hebrew culture, remembrance was not an individual or solitary function. People held something in memory in order to share it with others.

It is indeed possible that Mary served as Luke's source. According to ancient traditions, both were in Ephesus in the years soon after Jesus's ascension—Luke as a companion of St. Paul, and Mary in the care of St. John. It is inconceivable that a historian of Luke's rigor would have passed up an opportunity to preserve the only available oral history of Jesus's infancy.

In any event, Luke *does* provide detail that we do not find in the other Gospels. Only he tells the story of the angel's appearance to Mary.

> In the sixth month the angel Gabriel was sent from God to a city of Galilee named Nazareth, to a virgin betrothed to a man whose name was Joseph, of the house of David; and the virgin's name was Mary. And he came to her and said, "Hail, full of grace, the Lord is with you!" But she was greatly troubled at the saying, and considered in her mind what sort of greeting this might be. And the angel said to her, "Do not be afraid, Mary, for you have found favor with God. And behold, you will conceive in your womb and bear a son, and you shall call his name Jesus. He will be great, and will be called the Son of the Most
>   High;
> and the Lord God will give to him the throne of his father
>   David,
> and he will reign over the house of Jacob for ever;
> and of his kingdom there will be no end."
> And Mary said to the angel, "How shall this be, since I have no husband?" And the angel said to her,
> "The Holy Spirit will come upon you,
> and the power of the Most High will overshadow you;

therefore the child to be born will be called holy,
the Son of God.

And behold, your kinswoman Elizabeth in her old age has also conceived a son; and this is the sixth month with her who was called barren. For with God nothing will be impossible." And Mary said, "Behold, I am the handmaid of the Lord; let it be to me according to your word." And the angel departed from her. (Luke 1:26–38)

Luke's primary theological purpose is to account for the miracle of God's incarnation. Thus he is careful to establish Mary's virginity and to provide Mary's own testimony to the fact. Since Mary is a virgin, God is unquestionably the father of her child. The child is truly divine—and yet he is also truly human, gestating in the womb of a woman known to history.

Luke is attempting to account for an event unique in all of history. What Mary undergoes in this scene no other woman has ever undergone.

Mary's uniqueness is reflected in the angel's greeting to her. The angel says: "Hail, full of grace!" The Greek word the angel uses as a title for Mary, *kecharit men* , is a hapax, a singularity. It appears nowhere else in the Bible—and in fact, *nowhere else in Greek literature up to that time*. The English phrase "full of grace" shows up elsewhere in translations of the New Testament, but in those instances—for example, John 1:14 and Acts 6:8—it renders a different Greek phrase, *pleres charitos*. The title *kecharit men* is unique in the literary record because its owner and referent, Mary, is singular in human history.

As early as the third century, Christians remarked about this phenomenon. The great Scripture scholar Origen said: "The angel greeted Mary with a new address, which I could not find anywhere else in Scripture.... This greeting was reserved for Mary alone."[2] After its debut in the story of the annunciation, the word appears often in Christian texts, but always to describe or address the Blessed Virgin.

Because of its theological importance, Luke's account of the annunciation is cited in many works of the Fathers—Justin, Irenaeus, Origen, Ephrem, Cyril of Jerusalem, Gregory of Nyssa, Epiphanius, and others. Ambrose invokes the scene in order to explain what happens by the power of the Holy Spirit in the sacraments.[3]

The Fathers present Mary as a model of behavior for consecrated virgins especially, but also for ordinary Christians, as she seeks only to do the will of God. The imitation of Mary becomes an important theme in the preaching of the Fathers. "Learn of character from the Virgin. Learn of modesty from the Virgin. Learn of prophecy from the Virgin. Learn in the mystery."[4]

The Visitation

St. Luke goes on to relate Mary's visit to assist her elderly kinswoman Elizabeth, who is miraculously pregnant with John the Baptist. Elizabeth and her child both acknowledge the importance of Mary's baby, Elizabeth by calling him "Lord" (Luke 1:43) and John by leaping in the womb (1:44). Thus, faith in Jesus's divinity is shown to be a gift from God.

Origen surmises that Mary's holiness would have had a continued effect on Elizabeth and John:

The mere fact that Mary came to Elizabeth and greeted her made Elizabeth's infant "leap with joy" and made

"Elizabeth, filled with the Holy Spirit," prophesy those things which have been written in the Gospel. In one hour, Elizabeth made that much progress. We are left to conjecture what progress John made in the three months during which Mary dwelt with Elizabeth.

In a moment or an instant, the infant leapt up and, as it were, frolicked for joy, and Elizabeth was filled with the Holy Spirit. It would be most inappropriate if neither John nor Elizabeth profited from the immediate presence, for three months, of the Lord's mother and of the Savior himself.[5]

In the context of Mary's visitation with Elizabeth, we find her longest spoken address, known in the Western Church as the *Magnificat*, after the first word of its Latin translation:

My soul magnifies the Lord,
and my spirit rejoices in God my Savior,
for he has regarded the low estate of his handmaiden.
For behold, henceforth all generations will call me blessed;
for he who is mighty has done great things for me,
and holy is his name.
And his mercy is on those who fear him
from generation to generation.
He has shown strength with his arm,
he has scattered the proud in the imagination of their
    hearts,
he has put down the mighty from their thrones,
and exalted those of low degree;
he has filled the hungry with good things,

and the rich he has sent empty away.

He has helped his servant Israel,
   in remembrance of his mercy,
as he spoke to our fathers,
   to Abraham and to his posterity for ever. (Luke 1:46–55)

The *Magnificat*, as Luke presents it, has the qualities of Greek poetry. Yet it also follows the form of Hebrew songs and poems. Some scholars believe the Church used the text as a Marian hymn for years before Luke set down his Gospel. The Church has continued to do so. As early as the time of St. Benedict (sixth century), it has been part of the daily Evening Prayer in Benedictine monasteries.

In the *Magnificat*, Mary predicted, "All generations will call me blessed." And St. Luke would not have narrated Mary's words thus if they were not already true in his time. The Fathers represented the first generations to fulfill her prophecy. St. Jerome acclaimed her: "Holy Mary, blessed Mary, mother and virgin!"[6] On the strength of the *Magnificat*, some of the Fathers referred to Mary as "The Prophetess."[7] In her song, she foretold many events to come, through the generation of her Son and afterward.

The Savior Appears

Jesus's divinity is confirmed again in Luke's account of the child's miraculous birth, which is attended by angels (2:9–10, 13). Luke sets the scene of Jesus's nativity in Bethlehem, the predicted birthplace of the Messiah (see Micah 5:2), the anointed redeemer awaited by the Jews.

Perhaps no passages were so celebrated by the Fathers as those describing the nativity. They came to the fore especially as the feast of Christmas grew in popularity in the late fourth century.

From the nativity, St. Luke proceeds to the story of Jesus's presentation in the temple, which provides further testimonies to his identity as the Messiah. Jesus is recognized by Anna and Simeon, both pious and elderly Jews who possess the gift of prophecy. As Simeon blesses the Holy Family, he prophesies that Jesus "is set for the fall and rising of many in Israel, and for a sign that is spoken against" (2:34). Then he adds, to Mary, "And a sword will pierce through your own soul also, that thoughts out of many hearts may be revealed" (2:35).

Simeon's oracle is mysterious, and even the Fathers puzzled over its meaning. In the fourth century, St. Epiphanius thought it might be a prediction of Mary's death, though he wasn't willing to commit himself to that interpretation. A little earlier in the same century, St. Hilary of Poitiers marveled that even so great a figure as Mary should have to endure pain and suffering. What, he asked, can that mean for the rest of us?[8]

Later in Luke's second chapter appears the account of Jesus's separation from his family in Jerusalem when he was twelve years old. This story reinforces his divine origin and Mary's virginal conception, as Jesus himself identifies God as his Father, calling the temple "my Father's house" (2:49). At the end of the story, the reader learns that Jesus returned home and was obedient thereafter to Joseph and Mary, a fact that caused the Fathers to marvel: The Creator is subject to his creatures![9]

From Son to Master

The dynamic changed somewhat with Jesus's baptism in the River Jordan (see Luke 3:21–22). The Syriac Fathers—those who lived in lands that are today Iran and Iraq—noted a change in Jesus's relationships.[10] At the Jordan, they said, he passed from son to master. Mary, for her part, passed from mother to disciple.

In Luke's Gospel, Mary is never again called by name. She appears only in two curious episodes.

> Then his mother and his brethren came to him, but they could not reach him for the crowd. And he was told, "Your mother and your brethren are standing outside, desiring to see you." But he said to them, "My mother and my brethren are those who hear the word of God and do it." (Luke 8:19–21)

> A woman in the crowd raised her voice and said to him, "Blessed is the womb that bore you, and the breasts that you sucked!" But he said, "Blessed rather are those who hear the word of God and keep it!" (Luke 11:27–28)

Here we see Jesus subordinating his natural family to his supernatural family. If Mary is to be honored, she will be honored not primarily for her role in his conception and birth but rather because she heard the Word of God and kept it. The Fathers made much of this, going so far as to meditate on the virtues of the Blessed Virgin's ear.[11]

In the Gospels, taken as a whole, Mary emerges as the preeminent disciple. Though Peter denied him and Judas betrayed him, though James and John fell asleep in the garden, and all the others fled—Mary remained close to Jesus to the last.

The True Disciple

It is in the fourth Gospel, the Gospel according to St. John, that we see Mary at the foot of the cross. But earlier in that Gospel, we encounter her as a disciple among the disciples (see John 2:1–2). Whereas before, Jesus had been obedient to his parents, now his mother sets a standard of obedience for all who would benefit from her son's ministry. She says, "Do whatever he tells you" (John 2:5).

At the wedding feast in Cana of Galilee, the hosts run out of wine, and Mary intercedes with her son. Seemingly confident that he can and will put matters right, she simply points out the problem: "They have no wine" (2:3).

The Lord seems to rebuke her: "O woman, what have you to do with me? My hour has not yet come" (2:4). To the Fathers, Jesus's address seemed unusual for a son speaking to his mother—there is nothing like it in ancient literature. Yet it is the way Jesus typically spoke to women (see John 4:21). It indicates Mary's status now as his disciple—a supernatural relationship that is greater than natural bonds of kinship. St. Augustine wrote:

> He does not repel her, from whom he received the flesh, but means to convey the conception of his divinity with special fitness at this time, when he is about to change the water into wine. His divinity, likewise, had made that woman, and had not itself been made in her.[12]

Woman may also indicate Mary's special status in the new order established by her son. Readers since ancient times have noted that the opening of John's Gospel echoes the opening of the book of Genesis: "In the beginning..." There are many other echoes: a numbering of days, the Spirit hovering above the waters, and the introduction of "light" into the world. John presents Jesus's work as God's new act of creation. Jesus himself is the New Adam, and Mary appears as the New Eve. And "woman" is the literal meaning of Eve's name.

The New Eve motif is ubiquitous in the works of the Fathers, especially those of the earliest centuries. It will occupy us for an entire chapter a little later in this book. Here we merely observe it in passing.

Whereas St. Luke's Gospel presents Jesus's earthly origins, John begins with his heavenly birth: "In the beginning was the Word, and the Word was with God, and the Word was God,...the only-begotten Son, who is in the bosom of the Father" (John 1:1, 18). John's "infancy" narrative, in a sense, complements and completes Luke's. Or as St. Hilary put it, "I will not endure to hear that Christ was born of Mary unless I also hear 'In the beginning was the Word, and the Word was God.'"[13] Many of the Fathers made similar observations.

After the wedding feast at Cana, Jesus "went down to Capernaum, with his mother and his brethren and his disciples; and there they stayed for a few days" (John 2:12). And then Mary appears only once more in Jesus's public ministry, as a passing mention in a complaint by skeptical hearers: "The Jews then murmured at him, because he said, 'I am the bread which came down from heaven.' They said, 'Is not this Jesus, the son of Joseph, whose father and mother we know?'" (John 6:41–42). Here, those who reject Jesus's teaching on the gift of the Eucharist also fail to know the mystery of his virgin mother.

Mary reappears, however, at the crucial moment—at the foot of the cross.

> But standing by the cross of Jesus were his mother, and his mother's sister, Mary the wife of Clopas, and Mary Magdalene. When Jesus saw his mother, and the disciple whom he loved standing near, he said to his mother,

"Woman, behold, your son!" Then he said to the disciple, "Behold, your mother!" And from that hour the disciple took her to his own home. (John 19:25–27)

This is a key passage for the Marian spirit of the Fathers. In chapter one, we saw how it affected both Origen in the third century and Ambrose in the fourth. As Origen observed, John never names himself, using instead the phrase "disciple whom he loved." All Christians are invited to take that title for their own, identifying with St. John at the foot of the cross. And in doing so, they take Mary for their mother.

Matthew and Mark

Mary appears in St. Mark's Gospel hardly at all. Once we see Jesus's skeptical neighbors refer to him as "the Son of Mary" (Mark 6:3). They may have intended this as an insult. In Jesus's culture, it was customary to refer to a man as "son of" his father. Elsewhere in the Gospels, Jesus is called "the son of Joseph" (John 1:45; 6:42). It is possible that Mark's crowd is calling into question Jesus's legitimacy—and Mary's purity.

In one other place, Mark 3:31–35, we encounter Mary, in the scene we have already examined from Luke 8.

St. Matthew's Gospel is rich in Marian material. Like St. Luke, he presents the miracle of Jesus's conception and birth. But he presents it from the perspective of St. Joseph, who was engaged to be Mary's spouse. Mary is presented as a true though virginal spouse of Joseph.

Matthew begins his narrative with the genealogy of Jesus, at the end of which comes "Joseph the husband of Mary, of whom Jesus was born, who is called the Christ" (Matthew 1:16). Already, with this shift of language, Matthew indicates what is distinctive about the conception of Jesus. Each of the ancestors of Jesus "begot" their sons; yet Joseph is not spoken of as "begetting" his legal son, Jesus.

Matthew proceeds to elaborate on the consternation that Joseph felt upon discovering the pregnancy of Mary. The Fathers variously interpreted Joseph's decision to "send [Mary] away quietly" (Matthew 1:19). Some saw it as motivated by awe and reverence; others held that he suspected Mary of adultery; still others believed that he was perplexed by a situation that was beyond his powers of understanding.[14] In the end, Joseph's fears are resolved by a divine revelation of the nature of Mary's role in history. The angel of the Lord tells him:

> Joseph, son of David, do not fear to take Mary your wife, for that which is conceived in her is of the Holy Spirit; she will bear a son, and you shall call his name Jesus, for he will save his people from their sins. (Matthew 1:21)

Matthew, like Luke, takes care to specify that Mary was a virgin when she conceived: "When his mother Mary had been betrothed to Joseph, before they came together she was found to be with child of the Holy Spirit" (1:18). Joseph, Matthew tells us, "took his wife, but knew her not until she had borne a son" (1:24–25). In the fourth century, heretics would use the prepositions in these two sentences—*before* and *until*—to deny Mary's perpetual virginity. They were defeated by the arguments of St. Jerome, the great Scripture scholar and translator of the entire Bible.

The heresy emerged again a thousand years later, after the Protestant Reformation, though the original reformers, John

Calvin and Martin Luther, accepted the dogma of Mary's perpetual virginity as true and consonant with the Scriptures. We will return to this subject—and the Fathers' treatment of it—in chapter five, on Mary's virginity.

Matthew is the only evangelist to report the visit of the Magi from the East. These gentiles (non-Jews) were apparently righteous men seeking truth with human wisdom as they gazed at the stars. They could not have understood who the newborn "King of the Jews" really was. Yet they came "to worship him" (Matthew 2:2). The word *worship* here is the same word used by St. Matthew to describe the action of the disciples toward Jesus at the end of the Gospel (28:17). Remarkably, the Magi understood enough to recognize the transcendent mystery in the baby Jesus and worship him as God.

When at last the Magi reach Jesus, they find him with Mary, his mother. St. Joseph, who is usually more prominent in Matthew's account, mysteriously recedes into the background and is not mentioned in this scene. In the house where Mary sits, according to the Fathers, we see the image of the Church, whose center is Jesus.

The Early Church

Mary returns to the New Testament narrative at the beginning of the Church's life. It is Luke, again, who tells the story at the opening of his Acts of the Apostles. There are many parallels between the openings of Luke's Gospel and this later history. Both begin with Mary as she awaits the Holy Spirit. Luke, as a student of St. Paul, knew the Church to be the "body of Christ" (see 1 Corinthians 12:27; Ephesians 4:12). Just as Jesus's physical body was conceived by the power of the Spirit and through the willing prayers of Mary, so would his mystical body be conceived.

St. Paul, for his part, would show how Mary's role is essential to the proclamation of the Gospel:

> But when the time had fully come, God sent forth his Son, born of woman, born under the law, to redeem those who were under the law, so that we might receive adoption as sons. (Galatians 4:4–5)

The same concern arises in the later New Testament books attributed to St. John. Again and again, these emphasize the necessity of acknowledging "that Jesus Christ has come in the flesh" (1 John 4:2; see also 2 John 7). In proclaiming Mary's unique role—her virginal conception and motherhood—they establish the doctrine of the Incarnation: Jesus's true divinity with his true humanity.

The New Testament writers saw Adam as a "type" of Jesus Christ. As Adam was the prototype for humanity at the dawn of creation, so Jesus would serve as the model for redeemed humanity in the new creation. The Fathers unanimously and passionately believed that Eve was a type of the Virgin Mary. As woman, as virgin, and as mother, Eve foreshadowed the roles of Mary in the fullness of time.

But Eve did not exhaust the Old Testament types of Mary. The Fathers found the Virgin foreshadowed in many places. The Gospel of St. Matthew (1:23) cites the prophet Isaiah (7:14):

> "Behold, a virgin shall conceive and bear a son,
> and his name shall be called Emmanuel"
> (which means, God with us).

That passage is cited frequently in early Christian writings.

Jerome saw Mary as a fulfillment of the bride in the Song of Songs. He also placed Mary in the role of the queen in Psalm 45.

Gregory of Nyssa saw the Virgin Birth prefigured in the bush that Moses saw burning but not consumed.[15]

Typology shows the pattern of redemption as it is woven into the fabric of history and creation. God knew at the beginning how the story would end. The small details of the story point forward to history's resolution in the Savior, the cross, the empty tomb, and the Blessed Virgin.

The Woman of Revelation

A problematic passage for our consideration is the vision reported by John the seer in chapters eleven and twelve of the Book of Revelation:

> Then God's temple in heaven was opened, and the ark of his covenant was seen within his temple; and there were flashes of lightning, loud noises, peals of thunder, an earthquake, and heavy hail.
>
> And a great portent appeared in heaven, a woman clothed with the sun, with the moon under her feet, and on her head a crown of twelve stars; she was with child and she cried out in her pangs of birth, in anguish for delivery. And another portent appeared in heaven; behold, a great red dragon, with seven heads and ten horns, and seven diadems upon his heads. His tail swept down a third of the stars of heaven, and cast them to the earth. And the dragon stood before the woman who was about to bear a child, that he might devour her child when she brought it forth; she brought forth a male child, one who is to rule all the nations with a rod of iron, but her child was caught up to God and to his throne, and the woman fled into the wilderness, where she has a place prepared

by God, in which to be nourished for one thousand two hundred and sixty days....

And when the dragon saw that he had been thrown down to the earth, he pursued the woman who had borne the male child. But the woman was given the two wings of the great eagle that she might fly from the serpent into the wilderness, to the place where she is to be nourished for a time, and times, and half a time. The serpent poured water like a river out of his mouth after the woman, to sweep her away with the flood. But the earth came to the help of the woman, and the earth opened its mouth and swallowed the river which the dragon had poured from his mouth. (Revelation 11:19—12:1-6, 13-16)

When John speaks of "the woman," does he mean the Blessed Virgin Mary? Many of the Fathers seem to take the association for granted. They describe Mary as the Ark of the Covenant, for example, and they associate her with the baptismal rebirth of all Christians. The vision itself suggests many of the details of the life of Mary. The "woman" is the mother of the Messiah foretold in Psalm 2, the king who would rule with a rod of iron. The woman is forced to flee with her child, as Mary fled with Jesus to Egypt.

The problem is that none of the Fathers make the connection *explicitly* until the fourth century. St. Epiphanius is the first on record. Some earlier texts may allude to John's vision in their discussion of Mary, but it is impossible to say so with certainty.

The problem is compounded by the Fathers' skittishness about discussing the book of Revelation. Some use it extensively, and they are often the Fathers most effusive in their doctrine of Mary: Irenaeus and Origen, for example. Others, however, argued against its inclusion in the canon (St. Dionysius of Alexandria, for example). The Eastern Fathers especially treated the book with extreme reserve, and some local churches forbade its public proclamation.

The earliest commentators associated Revelation's "woman" with the Church. Yet these same Fathers often associated—indeed, *identified*—the Church with Mary.

Certainly the vision exercised a profound influence on Marian spirituality, doctrine, and art in later centuries of the Church's history. It is likely, as historians such as Blessed John Henry Newman have argued, that this interpretation followed earlier traditions that appear only obscurely in the surviving documents.

Newman drew his argument from a close reading of the Fathers, whose works he had translated from Greek and Latin. He observed that the vision, in the Bible's last book, revisited imagery from the opening chapters of the Bible's first book: "Not only mother and child, but a serpent is introduced into the vision. Such a meeting of man, woman, and serpent has not been found in Scripture, since the beginning of Scripture, and now it is found in its end."[16]

In Genesis, God foretells great conflict between the serpent and Eve's family. He says to the serpent:

> I will put enmity between you and the woman,
>> and between your seed and her seed;
> he shall bruise your head,
>> and you shall bruise his heel. (Genesis 3:15)

What is predicted in Genesis seems to be fulfilled vividly in the Apocalypse. Chapter twelve goes on to describe the serpent's enmity with the offspring of the woman: "Then the dragon was angry with the woman and went off to make war on the rest of her offspring, on those who keep the commandments of God and bear testimony to Jesus" (Revelation 12:17).

Many of the themes and symbols used in John's Gospel recur in the book of Revelation, which is also ascribed to John. In both, the author presents Jesus as the Lamb and the Word, titles not commonly used by the other New Testament writers. In the vision of Revelation, the seer could again be evoking a theme familiar from John's Gospel: the new creation, with its New Adam and New Eve—and now its serpent too.

CHAPTER THREE

OTHER SOURCES OF MARIAN DEVOTION ⁂

THE SCRIPTURES STAND IN A CATEGORY BY THEMSELVES AS primary sources of the Fathers' devotion. But they were not the only sources. In the earliest Christian centuries, there was a class of literature that mimicked the biblical books, expanded on biblical stories, and sometimes claimed biblical characters as their authors. In the decades immediately following the death of the last apostle, many such texts appeared. They bore suggestive titles like the Gospel of Thomas, the Acts of John, the Epistle of Barnabas, the Apocalypse of Peter, and the Odes of Solomon.

Scholars today refer to these books as *apocrypha*—which comes from the Greek word for "hidden"—or *pseudepigrapha*, from the Greek for "falsely ascribed." The latter term, though more difficult to pronounce, is the more accurate. *Apocrypha* can be misleading, as very few of the books were written to be hidden away. Quite the opposite, in fact: Their authors intended them to be bestsellers, popular books that answered the lingering questions of Christians who had already heard the authentic Christian Scriptures.

For example, the biblical Gospel of Luke states simply that the child Jesus was obedient to his parents as he grew up: "Jesus increased in wisdom and in stature, and in favor with God and man" (Luke 2:52). The infancy *pseudepigrapha*, however, fill out Jesus's young years with tales of a young wonderworker who brings his toys to life, strikes his neighbors dead, and withers the hand of his teacher. The Gospels of Matthew and Luke decorously assert that Mary was a virgin, but the *Infancy Gospel of James* brings in a midwife to conduct a physical examination.

These books are not authoritative, but they were widely influential. They don't reflect historical truth—most are extremely fanciful—but they're useful to us as indicators of the interests and piety of the early Christians. These were the bestsellers in an emerging market; some survive to our own day in hundreds of manuscripts from all over the ancient world.

Most were inspired, probably, by passionate devotion. In the year A.D. 190, Tertullian told the story of a priest in Asia who had recently been exposed as the author of *The Acts of Paul and Thecla*—and defrocked. The man confessed that he had written his fiction out of love for St. Paul.[1]

The books could inspire confusion as much as devotion. And since they were circulated under false names, no one was accountable for their contents. Some were simply tasteless and credulous; others were carefully wrought to justify heretical doctrines.

Another author of the 190s, Serapion, the bishop of Antioch, was shocked to find out that congregations were reading the *Gospel of Peter* in their liturgies. The text was probably produced by so-called *docetists*, heretics who believed that Jesus was not truly human but only seemed to be. Serapion wrote to his church: "Brethren, we receive Peter and the other apostles even as Christ; but the writings that go falsely by their names we, in our experience, reject, knowing that such things as these were never received."[2] Nevertheless, the books proliferated and accumulated. In the late fifth century, Pope Gelasius I decreed that nothing should be read in church except the canonical books of the Old and New Testaments. To his decree he appended an index of other Christian books, categorizing them according to their usefulness. He praised the decrees of the councils, the writings of the Fathers, and the ancient accounts of martyrdom. But then follows a long list of books and authors—more than a hundred all told—that Gelasius designated as "apocrypha." These, Gelasius said, "are to be avoided by Catholics."

The apocrypha on that list vary widely in orthodoxy, antiquity, and literary value. Some were written close to Gelasius's own time. Others were likely from the first century. Most fell somewhere in between. Though the Church had long since made a hard distinction between the canonical books and other pretenders, popular piety lagged behind. Christian demand kept the apocrypha in circulation at least until the late fifth century.

Some of the books on the Gelasian list contained material about the Blessed Virgin: "the book on the infancy of the Savior"; "the book of the Nativity of the Savior and of Mary or the midwife"; and "the book which is called the Assumption of Holy Mary." These and other titles certainly influenced many early Christians, and details sometimes show up in the sermons and poetry of the great Fathers. For those reasons, they deserve our attention now, at least for a brief introduction.

My Brother the Messiah

The Infancy Gospel of James is the most extensive, most influential, and probably the oldest trove of Marian material outside the pages of the New Testament. It purports to be written by James, "the Lord's brother" (Galatians 1:19), who in this telling is a son of Joseph from a previous marriage.

The Infancy Gospel of James was probably composed around A.D. 120. St. Justin Martyr, writing around 150, shows familiarity with its contents.

It begins by telling the story of the Blessed Virgin's birth and childhood. Ten of the book's twenty-four chapters are given to Mary's first twelve years. This is the oldest surviving text to name Mary's parents: Joachim and Anna. Like Zechariah and Elizabeth, they are elderly when their child is conceived. In gratitude, they dedicate her to God's service. From the time she is three, she lives in the temple, where the high priest assigns her to fashion cloth and veils for use in the temple liturgy. She is fed by the hand of an angel. From the time of Mary's betrothal onward, the document incorporates material from the early chapters of canonical Matthew and Luke, weaving the details together in a harmonious way.

The Infancy Gospel of James seems to have an apologetic purpose. The author assumes that readers might have a high degree of suspicion about Mary's virginal pregnancy, and so he provides many proofs. During her pregnancy, Mary and Joseph are made to undergo ordeals and tests, and they are vindicated repeatedly. As the time approaches for Mary to give birth, her midwife sees the baby appear miraculously and suddenly, without labor and without passing through the birth canal. A second midwife, who doubts her colleague's version of the recent events, conducts a physical examination and confirms that Mary's body is the same after birth as it was before conception.

The narrative continues with imaginative accounts of the baby's presentation in the temple and the flight from Herod. Zechariah, the priest married to Mary's kinswoman Elizabeth, dies a martyr's death in his efforts to save his child, John the Baptist.

The text of *The Infancy Gospel of James* indicates that the author was aware of Jewish temple traditions and very familiar with the Septuagint Greek translation of the Old Testament. Other texts from that time confirm that girls and young women served the temple in ways similar to those described in the account of Mary's childhood. *The Infancy Gospel of James* may have more historical value than other *pseudepigrapha*. The Fathers quote it more than any other.

Jesus's Childhood

The Infancy Gospel of Thomas claims to tell the story of Jesus from age five to age twelve, years missing from the canonical Gospels. The incidents are uniformly spectacular. At play at age five, Jesus purifies the waters in the local streams. He also fashions twelve sparrows out of clay. Joseph, his father, upbraids him for doing all this on a Sabbath. Jesus, in response, commands the sparrows to fly, and they obey him.

When the neighbor boys bully him or teachers give the young Messiah a hard time, they die or suffer physically. The neighbors attempt to evict the family, and Joseph cries out to Mary, "Do not let him go outside of the door, because those that make him angry die!" The text ends with an account of Jesus's separation from his family, based on the account in Luke's Gospel.

The Infancy Gospel of Thomas is also an early text, probably composed between A.D. 140 and 170. The story of the clay sparrows is repeated in some later sources.

There are other infancy gospels with the same sort of content as that of Thomas—Jesus, for example, turning playmates into goats. These were probably written centuries later than were Thomas and James. Their literary value is minimal, and their religious meaning almost nonexistent. They do, however, testify to the Christian public's continued demand for more and more information about Jesus. Even these sensationalist fictions were translated into many languages and survive in multiple manuscripts.

The Ascension of Isaiah

Possibly the earliest of the non-canonical infancy accounts is the one embedded in *The Ascension of Isaiah*, a text of the mid to late first century.[3] Its origins, authorship, and composition are much debated. It seems to include Jewish traditions about the Old Testament prophet and Christian traditions about Jesus (some of which we have encountered in *The Infancy Gospel of James*). Both Justin Martyr and the author of the New Testament Letter to the Hebrews seem to be aware of material that is peculiar to *The Ascension of Isaiah*.

In Chapter 11, "Isaiah" sets down a vision of the birth of the Messiah, which he foresees from a heavenly vantage point:

> And I indeed saw a woman of the family of David the prophet, named Mary, and Virgin, and she was espoused to a man named Joseph, a carpenter, and he also was of the seed and family of the righteous David of Bethlehem Judah. And he came into his lot. And when she was espoused, she was found with child, and Joseph the carpenter was desirous to put her away.
>
> But the angel of the Spirit appeared in this world, and after that Joseph did not put her away, but kept Mary and did not reveal this matter to any one. And he did not approach Mary, but kept her as a holy virgin, though

with child. And he did not live with her for two months. And after two months of days while Joseph was in his house, and Mary his wife, but both alone.

It came to pass that when they were alone that Mary straight-way looked with her eyes and saw a small babe, and she was astonished. And after she had been astonished, her womb was found as formerly before she had conceived.

And when her husband Joseph said unto her: "What has astonished you?" his eyes were opened and he saw the infant and praised God, because into his portion God had come. And a voice came to them: "Tell this vision to no one."

And the story regarding the infant was noised broad in Bethlehem. Some said: "The Virgin Mary has borne a child, before she was married two months." And many said: "She has not borne a child, nor has a midwife gone up (to her), nor have we heard the cries of (labor) pains." And they were all blinded respecting Him and they all knew regarding Him..., though they knew not whence He was.

And they took Him, and went to Nazareth in Galilee.[4]

The text is important for many reasons. It shows a very early concern to defend Mary's virginity not only before and during conception but also during and after birth. If *The Ascension of Isaiah* was indeed produced between A.D. 70 and 80, as scholarly consensus indicates, then it would seem that Mary's perpetual virginity was well established by the first generation after Pentecost.

Odes of Solomon

Liturgical material represents another category of sources for the Fathers' Marian preaching. We possess the texts of blessings, Eucharistic prayers, and many hymns and antiphons. Among the earliest and most intriguing are the so-called *Odes of Solomon*. Attributed to Israel's wise king, the *Odes* may have been composed piecemeal from the first century through the third. The hymns that deal with Mary have been plausibly dated to the first century.[5]

In Ode 19, we find many themes that should, by now, be familiar: Mary's conception of Jesus by the power of the Holy Spirit, her miraculous delivery, and her tender motherhood.

> [The Spirit] opened the womb of the Virgin and she received conception and brought forth; and the Virgin became a Mother with many mercies; And she travailed and brought forth a Son, without incurring pain;
>
> And because she was not sufficiently prepared, and she had not sought a midwife (for He brought her to bear), she brought forth, as if she were a man, of her own will; And she brought Him forth openly, and acquired Him with great dignity,
>
> And loved Him in his swaddling clothes, and guarded Him kindly, and showed Him in Majesty. Hallelujah![6]

In a later Ode (33), we find ambiguous language that could refer to the Blessed Virgin or to the Church—or to both as terms somehow symbolic of one another. This last approach is one taken increasingly by the Fathers as the centuries passed.

> But there stood a perfect virgin who was proclaiming and calling and saying,

"O sons of men, return, and you daughters of men,
   come:
And forsake the ways of that corruption and draw
   near."[7]

Oracles

There is still another strain of pseudonymous sources for the early Church's Marian devotion. It is the curious genre of prophecies attributed to pagan seers. The most famous collection of these is the *Sibylline Oracles*, named for the prophetesses (Sibyls) who spoke for various gods of Greek mythology. The Sibyls followed strict poetic form in their utterances, which were given in a trance or frenzy.

The oracles that survive represent a variety of religious traditions—pagan, Christian, and Jewish. The first two books of the standard collection appear to have been written or edited by Christians. In our first chapter, we mentioned one of several recorded instances of favors won through the Virgin Mary's intercession.[8] Marian material appears also in oracles that describe the Lord's incarnation.

But in the latest times the earth he passed,
And coming late from the Virgin Mary's womb
A new light rose, and going forth from heaven
Put on a mortal form. First then did Gabriel show
His strong pure form; and bearing his own news
He next addressed the maiden with his voice:
"O virgin, in thy bosom undefiled
Receive thou God." Thus speaking he inbreathed
God's grace on the sweet maiden; and straightway
Alarm and wonder seized her as she heard,

And she stood trembling; and her mind was wild
With flutter of excitement while at heart
She quivered at the unlooked-for things she heard.
But she again was gladdened and her heart
Was cheered by the voice, and the maiden laughed
And her cheek reddened with a sense of joy,
And spell-bound was her heart with sense of shame.
And confidence came to her. And the Word
Flew into the womb, and in course of time
Having become flesh and endued with life
Was made a human form and came to be
A boy distinguished by his virgin birth;
For this was a great wonder to mankind,
But it was no great wonder unto God
The Father, nor was it to God the Son.
And the glad earth received the newborn babe,
The heavenly throne laughed and the world rejoiced.
And the prophetic new-appearing star
Was honored by the wise men, and the babe
Born was shown in a manger unto them
That obeyed God, and keepers of the herds,
And goatherds and to shepherds of the lambs.[9]

Why would the early Christians have cast such beautiful poetry as pagan oracles? Some Christian thinkers—such as Justin Martyr in the mid-second century—believed that God had prepared the way of the Messiah not only in Israel but also among the gentiles. Justin spoke of God's planting in creation "seeds of the Word," evidence of his divine existence and action. He also held that all "who lived reasonably are Christians,"[10] even pagan philosophers like Socrates. Justin argued—or hoped—that God would enlighten all sincere seekers of truth.

The same idea would appear later, as the "preparation for the Gospel," in Eusebius and others. Such is the generous spirit that pervades the *Sibylline Oracles*.

Traditions

There were oral traditions too associated with Mary, and we see these emerge in the works of the earliest Fathers. From St. Ignatius of Antioch, for example, we learn of three secrets that were kept hidden from Satan.

> Now the virginity of Mary was hidden from the prince of this world, as was also her offspring, and the death of the Lord; three mysteries of renown, which were wrought in silence by God.[11]

Ignatius so esteemed the virginity of Mary as a work of God that he placed it in relation to the central mysteries of Christianity, Jesus's incarnation and his redemptive death. Implicit perhaps is the fulfillment of Genesis 3:15, as the woman is at enmity with the devil. Ignatius then proceeds to give a stylized description of the advent of Jesus and its effects on the cosmos.

> How, then, was he manifested to the world? A star shone forth in heaven above all the other stars, the light of which was inexpressible, while its novelty struck men with astonishment. And all the rest of the stars, with the sun and moon, formed a chorus to this star, and its light was exceedingly great above them all. And there was agitation felt as to whence this new spectacle came, so unlike to everything else [in the heavens].

Hence every kind of magic was destroyed, and every bond of wickedness disappeared; ignorance was removed, and the old kingdom abolished, God himself being manifested in human form for the renewal of eternal life.[12]

The sun, moon, and stars here are reminiscent of the vision in the New Testament book of Revelation, where they also seem to describe the coming of the Savior. Similar cosmic imagery arises a century later with St. Hippolytus of Rome, who describes "the blessed apostles, together with Mary and Joseph," bowing down before Jesus and compares them to "the sun and the moon and the eleven stars" bowing down in the vision of the patriarch Joseph (see Genesis 37:9).[13] Associating the Blessed Virgin Mary with the sun—along with the apostles as merely stars—suggests an immense esteem for the holiness and dignity of Mary (and a remarkable appreciation of St. Joseph, her spouse).

Justin Martyr also spoke of traditions related to the sites associated with Mary's life. Justin had grown up in Palestine at the turn of the second century, and he knew of the location of the cave of the nativity—which had by then been repurposed by the Romans—because of the tradition preserved by residents of Bethlehem.[14] Justin's traditions are confirmed by Origen a century later, when he makes his own pilgrimage to Bethlehem.[15]

Ignatius, Justin, and Hippolytus allude to traditions they presume their readers or hearers will understand. Today we retain what these forgotten traditions served to promote. We venerate Mary, and staying close to her, we are close to our ancestors in the faith.

CHAPTER FOUR

HER NAME ✠

IN EVERY YEAR FROM 1900 TO 1946, MARY WAS THE MOST popular name given to girls born in the United States. In many of those years, variants—such as Marie—also occupied positions in the top ten. From 1947 to 1952, Mary slipped to second place before regaining the upper spot from 1953 to 1961. It remained in the first five till 1967 but has not returned since then.[1]

Mary (with its variants) seems to have also been the most popular name for girls in first-century Palestine. Some scholars estimate that the name was held by more than 25 percent of the female population! It is the most common female name in the New Testament. The Gospels tell of Mary of Magdala (Mary Magdalene) (Luke 8:2), Mary of Bethany (Luke 10:38–42), Mary the mother of James and Joses (Mark 15:40), and Mary the wife of Clopas (John 19:25). In Acts, we encounter Mary the mother of John Mark (Acts 12:12), and in Paul's Letter to the Romans (16:6), we meet a hardworking Mary among the Christians in the capital city. And of course, Mary is the name of Jesus's mother.

Mariamne (a variant) was the name of the second and third wives of King Herod the Great. The name was commonly given in the royal house from the first century B.C. through the first century A.D.—and many ordinary Jewish families took up the practice. The name appears frequently in documents and inscriptions associated with Jews from the period, in contracts and correspondence, on receipts and on tombstones. In Hebrew it is *Miryam* or *Miriam*, which is rendered in Greek and Latin as *Maria*.

It's hard to know what accounts for the popularity of the name, though the royal association certainly didn't hurt. The name does not appear as often in the centuries before the birth of the Blessed Virgin.

Miriam

The earliest recorded occurrence of the name is in the book of Exodus. Miriam, the sister of Moses and Aaron, is identified as "the prophetess" (Exodus 15:20). She and her brothers governed as a triumvirate. It was she who sang the song of victory at the Exodus:

> Sing to the Lord, for he has triumphed gloriously;
>   the horse and his rider he has thrown into the sea.
> (Exodus 15:21)

Miriam is permanently associated with her brothers and their heroic deeds (see Micah 6:4). Yet the name Miriam is given to just one other person mentioned in the Old Testament (1 Chronicles 4:17)—and it's a male!

The story of Moses's sister Miriam is mixed. She had the gift of prophecy, and she exercised governance—an extremely rare thing for a woman in the ancient world. But she also rebelled against Moses because he took a foreign woman in marriage, and God punished her with leprosy (see Numbers 12). As a result, her name stood as a cautionary tale against wrongdoing and rebellion: "Remember what the Lord your God did to Miriam on the way as you came forth out of Egypt" (Deuteronomy 24:9).

Yet Miriam's reputation in folklore was overwhelmingly positive. The rabbis saw her as a champion of family unity. In one story commonly retold, when Pharaoh decrees that all the Israelite male children must be drowned in the Nile River, Miriam's father despairs, divorces his wife, and abandons the family. Miriam, then just a young girl, finds him and reproaches him for his lack of faith in God's providence. The man returns home, remarries his wife, and soon fathers Moses, the deliverer of Israel.

Many of the rabbis believed that Miriam was one of the Hebrew midwives who rescued babies, including her brother Moses (see Exodus 1:15–21). In legends, Miriam is also commonly associated with the Israelites' ability to find water in the desert.

It is possible that such legendary material accounts for the increase in the popularity of the name Miriam—Mary—in the first century before Christ and afterward. In a time of cultural subjection, it was, perhaps, an act of hope for Israel's deliverance once again, in the coming generation.

As Moses's sister was called "Miriam the prophetess" in the Old Testament, so Mary was called "Miriam the prophetess" by the Fathers of the Syriac tradition, who spoke the language of Jesus.[2] Both women spoke few words in their oracles but all to mighty effect.

What's in a Name?

All words—said Ralph Waldo Emerson—are fossil poetry.[3] For the ancients, that was doubly true of names. For Israelites and gentiles alike, there was nothing arbitrary about a person's name. It represented destiny. Eve is so named "because she was the mother of all living" (Genesis 3:20). Ishmael is so named "because the Lord has given heed to your affliction" (Genesis 16:11). Jesus is so named because "he will save his people from their sins" (Matthew 1:21).

The ancients savored names and assigned them enormous signif-icance. Socrates declared that "names rightly given are the like-nesses and images of the things which they name" and "the name is an imitation of the thing."[4] The Jewish philosopher Philo, a contemporary of Jesus, agreed with that principle and drew elab-orate allegories out of what he guessed to be the origins of biblical names. Etymology was largely creative guesswork, honored as much for its cleverness as for its science.

The meaning of *Mary* has been debated since ancient times. For the early rabbis, the name Miriam reflected the bitterness (*mirur*) of Israel's enslavement by the Egyptians. St. Jerome, following after Origen and Eusebius, believed the name to mean "drop from the sea" or "myrrh of the sea."[5] Other proposed etymologies range from the simple to the silly: "rebellious one," or "corpulent one," or "wished-for child." To the later Fathers—who knew no Hebrew—it could only represent ideals, such as "lady," "beau-tiful one," or "beloved of God."

Around the time of Christ, Philo of Alexandria fashioned an alle-gorical interpretation of the Old Testament Miriam, her name, and her office. To him she represented "the purified outward sense." Philo was a Jew, not a Christian, but to the early Christians (who knew his writings well), his analysis must have seemed prophetic.

> And the chorus of men will have Moses for their leader; and that of the women will be under the guidance of Miriam, "the purified outward sense." For it is just that hymns and praises should be uttered in honor of God without any delay, both in accordance with the sugges-tions of the intellect and the perceptions of the outward senses...in gratitude and honor to the holy Savior.

Accordingly, all the men sing the song on the seashore, not indeed with a blind mind, but seeing sharply, Moses being the leader of the song; and women sing, who are in good truth the most excellent of their sex, having been enrolled in the lists of the republic of virtue, Miriam being their leader.[6]

Respect for the Name

In *The Infancy Gospel of James*, the temple's high priest blesses Mary with the words: "The Lord has magnified your name in all generations."[7] In the fourth century, St. Ephrem of Syria would sing to Mary: "Blessed are you...whose name is great and exalted because of your child."[8]

Her "name" is to be great and exalted, and yet there is in the earliest Christians a discernible reticence about mentioning her name at all. John's Gospel does not use Mary's name. In the other Gospels, it appears only in the infancy narratives and when skeptics inquire about Jesus's background (see Matthew 13:55; Mark 6:3). In some manuscripts of the Acts of the Apostles, she is "the mother of Jesus." In Paul's Letter to the Galatians, she is simply "woman" (4:4).

This reticence is reflected even in the habits of Christian scribes. The text critic Larry Hurtado notes that the early Christians, following Jewish practice, preferred not to spell out names that were deemed sacred.[9] In Jesus's time, Jews were forbidden to write or pronounce the name of God. Only the temple's high priest could utter it—and even he could say it only once a year, on the Day of Atonement, when he stood in the Holy of Holies. Thus, in manuscripts, God's name was rendered by its four consonants, with no vowels: YHWH.

Christians seem to have kept this scribal norm—and extended it to those few biblical figures who had come to share God's life with a certain fullness. *Kyrios*, the Greek word for "Lord," was usually abbreviated to its first and last letters. *Iesous* (Jesus) similarly was shortened to its first two letters. *Huious* (Son) was abbreviated, but only when it referred to Jesus. The names of Moses and Elijah—both of whom had been taken to heaven at the end of their early days—were also treated in this way.

And so was the name of Mary. In fact, so was the word *Meter* (Mother), *but only when it referred to Mary*. In the Ethiopian tradition, we find a similar custom of featuring Mary's name in red letters, an honor usually given only to the name of God.[10]

Writing on the Walls

The name Mary was rarely used in gentile lands at the time of Christ. There are a few—but only a few—instances of its use among the Romans. But with the spread of the Christian faith, the name became very common throughout the Greco-Roman world. At the same time, it retained its popularity among Jews, who were, after A.D. 135, exiled from the lands of Israel.

The name of Mary was magnified in new ways, including Christian graffiti, which appears at pilgrimage sites from the Holy Land to Italy. On a column from an early Christian synagogue in Nazareth, some ancient pilgrim scratched the Greek words for "Hail Mary." Near the same place, another Christian wrote the self-evident statement: "On the holy site of M I have written."[11] Both ancient testimonies are preserved and visible for pilgrims today. In some graffiti, Mary's initials MA are overlaid with the initial of her son, X, to make a pleasing geometric pattern.

In the remains of ancient Rome, *Mary* appears often in scrawls and inscriptions. In fact, Mary is the only saint whose tributes rival the founders of the Roman Church, Peter and Paul. Most of the graffiti are tributes or simple requests for intercession. Some, however, are more creative. At the original tomb of St. Peter—which was only recently excavated—Mary's name appears merged with the Greek word for "victory," as if they represent closely related terms.[12]

And they do. The oldest Marian hymn we know, the so-called "Hymn Against Marcion," tells us that in Jesus, "a man from virgin born proved to be the victor."[13]

What we see abbreviated in the words scratched on plaster—and what we hear in the ancient hymn—we read in the fourth-century sermons of St. Ambrose of Milan. He rebuked Satan with the *name* of the Virgin: "Mary conquered you as she gave birth to the Victor…who when crucified would defeat you and when dead would bring you into subjection. You will be conquered today so that the woman should defeat your attacks."[14]

CHAPTER FIVE

THE VIRGIN ✠

THE EVANGELISTS, AS THEY WROTE THE GOSPELS OF THE NEW
Testament, were clearly concerned about establishing Mary's
virginity. The authors of the apocrypha sometimes seem obsessed
with it. It figures too in the writings of many of the early Fathers.

Few themes, in fact, are so ubiquitous in ancient Christian literature as the virginal conception and miraculous birth of Jesus. It
is everywhere in the Christian sources because it is a hinge of true
doctrine. Mary's virginity is proof of God's fatherhood of Jesus—
and so it is a proof of Jesus's divinity.

It is likely, however, that there were other, negative reasons
for the first Christians' frequent return to this theme. The most
ancient sources suggest that the doctrine of Mary's virginity was a
favorite target of the Church's enemies. Many scholars believe the
New Testament infancy narratives were crafted, at least in part,
as a response to Jewish opponents who disputed Christian claims
about miracles.

Matthew acknowledges that false stories were "spread among
the Jews" in his day (see Matthew 28:13–15). Though Matthew is
specifically concerned with disinformation regarding Jesus's resurrection, it is clear from other ancient literature that Mary's reputation was also called into question. There is abundant evidence of
this in both Jewish and pagan sources.

Attacks on the Mother

The Talmud, first set down in writing around the year A.D. 200, is a collection of older Jewish traditions that became, according to the historian Peter Schäfer, "the defining document of those who refused to accept the new covenant."[1] Thus its teachings include sometimes subtle, and sometimes explicit, rejections of Christian doctrine, including slurs on the character of Jesus and that of Mary. Schäfer—who is director of Princeton University's program in Judaic Studies—explains:

> The rabbis drafted…a powerful counternarrative that was meant to shake the foundations of the Christian message: for, according to them, Jesus was not born from a virgin, as his followers claimed, but out of wedlock, the son of a whore and her lover; therefore, he could not be the Messiah of Davidic descent, let alone the Son of God.[2]

Schäfer's summary is shocking, but it is a fair assessment of the material. Mary appears in the Talmud "not in a coherent narrative, but scattered throughout the rabbinic literature in general and the Talmud in particular and often dealt with in passing."[3] The assertions are uniformly insulting to Mary as well as Jesus.

It is indisputable too that these slurs were part of a stock anti-Christian apologetic long before the Talmud was compiled. Already in the year A.D. 138, the pagan pamphleteer Celsus marshaled many of the same stories for his own attack on Christianity. He cites his source simply as "a Jew." Celsus imagines such a Jew confronting Jesus and demanding an account of his origins:

> Is it not true, good sir, that you fabricated the story of your birth from a virgin to quiet rumors about the true

and unsavory circumstances of your origins? Is it not the
case that far from being born in the royal David's city of
Bethlehem, you were born in a poor country town, and
of a woman who earned her living by spinning? Is it not
the case that when her deceit was uncovered, to wit, that
she was pregnant by a Roman soldier called Panthera,
she was driven away by her husband—the carpenter—
and convicted of adultery?[4]

Christianity's enemies clearly perceived Mary's virginity as a weak
point of the Christian argument. While miracles serve to confirm
the faith of eyewitnesses, they can seem absurd to others who are
skeptical. Miracles, by definition, run counter to ordinary human
experience. Skeptics need only respond with a raised eyebrow or a
smirk—or the literary equivalent of these facial expressions—and
they've made their case.

To the Jews' objections, Celsus added his own. He said that the
story of Jesus's conception was simply a rehash of pagan myths
about gods impregnating human women. He added, moreover,
that Mary seemed extremely unlikely to attract a god, since "she
was neither rich nor of royal rank."[5]

The constancy of the Christian witness to Mary's virginity
probably reflects the vehemence of the attacks from non-Christians.
If *The Infancy Gospel of James* breaches decorum by introducing
the alleged testimony of a midwife, it is because the author
believed such "evidence" could convince opponents or reassure
troubled believers.

St. Justin Martyr wrote that Jews in his time also argued that
Isaiah's Emmanuel oracle (7:14), cited by St. Matthew, did not
really predict that "a *virgin* shall conceive and bear a son" but
rather that "a *young woman* shall conceive."[6] In Hebrew, as in

other languages, the word for a young woman can also stand as a euphemism for a woman who is sexually virginal. (Consider the German word *jungfrau* and the archaic English *maiden*. The cultural assumption behind these is that an unmarried person is sexually inexperienced.)

Justin responds simply that the oracle, delivered by Isaiah with great rhetorical force, makes no sense if it's speaking of a woman who is not a virgin. St. Cyril of Jerusalem will deliver the same argument, in greater detail, in the fourth century. Isaiah promises the king a "sign," and a young woman getting pregnant is simply not a sign. A virginal conception, however, is a sign worthy of Isaiah's dramatic crescendo.[7] Isaiah had, after all, prompted Ahaz to ask for a sign "as deep as Sheol or high as heaven" (Isaiah 7:10).

Two centuries had passed between Justin and Cyril, and yet Christians were responding with the same answers to the same charges from their opponents. We should perhaps not be surprised when hostile media recycle the ancient arguments in the weeks leading up to next Christmas.

The Rule of Faith

Within the Church, Mary's virginity was an essential element of catechesis. It was one of those few basic truths that served as the norm of Christian faith. Sometimes these truths were preached in summary form, called the "rule of faith" or "canon of truth." You can find examples in the works of many of the early Fathers, like this one from St. Irenaeus in the mid-100s.

> The Church, though dispersed throughout the whole world, even to the ends of the earth, has received from the apostles and their disciples this faith: [She believes]

in one God, the Father Almighty, Maker of heaven, and earth, and the sea, and all things that are in them; and in one Christ Jesus, the Son of God, who became incarnate for our salvation; and in the Holy Spirit, who proclaimed through the prophets the dispensations of God, and the advents, and the birth from a virgin.[8]

Such is the faith of the Church—and it affirms Jesus's "birth from a virgin." Tertullian puts it emphatically: "The rule of faith, indeed, is altogether one, alone immovable and irreformable; the rule, to wit, of believing in one only God omnipotent, the Creator of the universe, and his Son Jesus Christ, born of the Virgin Mary."[9]

Even when addressing pagans, Christians did not avoid the "scandal" of Mary's virginal maternity. A remarkable summary of the faith comes from Aristides the philosopher, an Athenian sage in the early second century. In testimony to the Emperor Hadrian, Aristides described Mary's role as virgin and mother:

The Christians, then, trace the beginning of their religion from Jesus the Messiah; and he is named the Son of God Most High. And it is said that God came down from heaven, and from a Hebrew virgin assumed and clothed himself with flesh; and the Son of God lived in a daughter of man.[10]

Eventually, the primitive "rule of faith" coalesced into creeds, brief fixed formulas that summarize the key tenets of Christianity. The creeds used in the Catholic liturgy today—the Apostles' Creed and the Nicene Creed—both have roots in the early Church. And both affirm that Jesus, the Son of God, was "born" or "incarnate" "of the Virgin Mary."

The creeds do not mention the apostles Peter and Paul, important as those men were to the ongoing life of the Church. But they do mention Mary, and they mention her as "the Virgin." To proclaim the gospel, the Church found it necessary to proclaim Mary alongside her divine Son—to *name* her—and to insist upon her virginal motherhood.

The doctrines affirmed in the creeds are there because someone—or some group—opposed them in ancient times. In the face of heresy or opposition, it became necessary for Christians to take a stand, to profess belief in the very doctrines that were under attack. That was true of Jesus's divinity, which is affirmed in the creeds. That was true of Jesus's humanity, which is affirmed in the creeds. It is true as well of Mary's virginal motherhood, which is a safeguard and proof of her Son's divinity and humanity.

Model of Virgins

Mary's virginity was not merely admired in the Church; it was also imitated. St. Paul, in his First Letter to the Corinthians, speaks of Christians who consecrated themselves to lifelong virginity and celibacy (see 1 Corinthians 7). Paul himself lived this way, as did Jesus before him. Jesus declared that some are called to give themselves entirely to God, apart from married life (Matthew 19:12; Mark 10:29–30).

Later in the first century, consecrated virgins and celibates were already a fixture in the Church. Both Clement of Rome and Ignatius of Antioch mention them, warning only that they should not allow themselves to become proud of their exalted place in the community. "Let him who is continent not boast of it," said Clement. "Know that it is another who gives the power of continence."[11] Ignatius added, "If anyone is able to remain continent, to the honor of the Flesh of the Lord, let him persistently avoid boasting."[12]

By the middle of the second century, consecrated virgins were a distinguishing mark of the Christian Church. Even the pagans marveled at the phenomenon. The pagan physician Galen remarked that Christians accomplished the kind of self-control that Stoic philosophers theorized about.[13] St. Athenagoras of Athens wrote to Marcus Aurelius that he "would find *many* among us, both men and women, growing old unmarried, in hope of living in closer communion with God."[14] He did not hesitate to use the word *many* when he spoke of Christian virgins, widows, and celibates. In Antioch in the time of St. John Chrysostom, there were 3,000 consecrated virgins and widows in a city whose population was 250,000.

In the writings of the Fathers, Mary emerged consistently as the model for such consecrated lives. Athanasius, Basil, Ambrose, Jerome, and Augustine all addressed important works to communities of consecrated women, and all of them dwelt upon the example of Mary. St. Ambrose said, "Let the life of Mary be like an image of virginity itself.... From this you may take your pattern of life."[15] Indeed, St. Augustine argued that Mary had taken a vow of virginity even before her visit from the angel, as did St. Gregory of Nyssa:

> What is Mary's response? Listen to the voice of the pure Virgin. The angel brings the glad tidings of childbearing, but she is concerned with virginity and holds that her integrity should come before the angelic message. She does not refuse to believe the angel; neither does she move away from her convictions. She says: I have given up any

contact with man. "How will this happen to me, since I do not know man?" (Luke 1:34)...[I]f Joseph had taken her to be his wife, for the purpose of having children, why would she have wondered at the announcement of maternity, since she herself would have accepted becoming a mother according to the law of nature?[16]

From the details of Mary's life—as preached in the Fathers—consecrated virgins learned the virtues of loyalty, chastity, humility, industry, piety, and contemplation. They learned to be perfect disciples of Jesus after the model of the first and most perfect disciple.

In Defense of the Virgin

The early Church honored Mary as "Ever Virgin." In the fourth century, the title appears in St. Ambrose among the Latins and St. Amphilochius among the Greeks. With or without the title, the idea of Mary's perpetual virginity is everywhere. The Fathers believed that Mary was a virgin when she conceived, that she remained physically virginal in giving birth, and that afterward she preserved her virginity for the rest of her life.

The early texts, such as the *Odes of Solomon* and *The Infancy Gospel of James*, assert that Mary suffered no childbirth pangs. They describe Jesus's passing through her as light passes through a window. St. Jerome compared this passing from Mary to Jesus's passing through walls on the days after his resurrection (see John 20:19, 26).[17]

"Lovers of Christ," said St. Basil, "cannot hear that the Mother of God ever ceased to be a virgin."[18] This is the overwhelming consensus of the Fathers: that Mary and Joseph, by mutual consent, never physically consummated their marriage.

Among the authors of the early Church, Tertullian of Carthage is the only dissenting voice. (When a heretic of the fourth century cited the North African as his authority in this matter, St. Jerome noted caustically that Tertullian also left the Church.) Tertullian claimed that Mary's labor and childbirth were physically no different from any other woman's.[19] He offered scriptural reasons for saying so, but his primary purpose was to oppose the Gnostic heretics in their disdain for the human body. He believed that Jesus's true humanity depended upon a normal birth.

In his zeal—in this matter as in others—Tertullian overshot the mark of truth and ran to the opposite error. He may also have believed that the "brethren" of the Lord mentioned in the Gospels (Matthew 13:55; Mark 6:3) were younger children of Mary and Joseph. His claims about this are less clear (and thus less clearly contrary to Tradition) than his claims about Jesus's birth.

Not till the end of the fourth century was there any serious challenge to the doctrine of Mary's perpetual virginity. Then arose Bonosus, bishop of Sardica, and Helvidius, an Italian writer, who opposed it for various reasons. Helvidius's intention may have been to restore the honor of marriage at a time when virginity was much in vogue. But like Tertullian, he sought to overturn a longstanding and important tradition in order to make a slight correction. It was his lot to attract the attention of the greatest Scripture scholar of his time, St. Jerome—who was also famous for his volatile temper.

Jerome responded with his tract *Against Helvidius*. It is an argument in the technical sense—a persuasive ordering of reasons and evidence. But it is also an argument in the popular sense—a heated, passionate disagreement. Jerome responds with scholarship but also with the anger of a man whose enemies have dared to insult his mother.

Helvidius's arguments rested on his reading of the two texts cited earlier, from the first chapter of St. Matthew's Gospel:

> When his mother Mary had been betrothed to Joseph, *before* they came together she was found to be with child of the Holy Spirit.... When Joseph woke from sleep, he did as the angel of the Lord commanded him; he took his wife, but knew her not *until* she had borne a son. (Matthew 1:18, 24–25, emphases added)

Helvidius contended that both *before* and *until* in these passages imply a time "after," when conditions would be different than they had been at first. Jerome, by far the superior linguist, used Scriptural texts to demonstrate the logical incoherence of his opponent's position.

> What then does [Paul] mean by saying, "for he must reign, till he has put all enemies under his feet" (1 Corinthians 15:25)? Is the Lord to reign only until his enemies begin to be under his feet, and once they are under his feet will he cease to reign?[20]

Jerome multiplied the citations from Holy Writ and added some original examples to insult his opponent: "Helvidius, *before* he repented, was cut off by death."[21]

Jerome also schooled Helvidius in the Semitic use of *brother* to describe a wide range of kinship. History records nothing more of Helvidius. St. Ambrose's refutation of Bonosus is less memorable, perhaps, but no less devastating to the arguments against Mary's virginity.

CHAPTER SIX

THE NEW EVE 🔆

BLESSED JOHN HENRY CARDINAL NEWMAN IS WIDELY ACKNOWL-edged as one of the great scholars of Christian origins. He began his academic career as a Protestant, in the evangelical wing of the Anglican Church. While still a young man, he produced many translations and studies of the early Fathers. He taught Church history at Oxford.

At midlife, Newman became a Roman Catholic, and in a letter to his closest friend and colleague, he tried to give an account of his conversion to the communion he called "the Church of the Fathers." Like many Protestants, his friend objected to Catholic devotion to Mary, claiming that it had little precedent in the early Church. Newman responded with a book's worth of evidence.

Newman begins at the beginning of Church history, with what he identifies as "the great rudimental teaching of Antiquity from its earliest date" concerning Mary. And that is the doctrine—or rather motif—of the New Eve.

Newman calls many witnesses to the stand, and today he could have called more, as many other texts have become available since the mid-nineteenth century. Yet his roster, as it stands, is an impressive array of the leading lights of early Christianity: Justin, Irenaeus, Tertullian, Cyril of Jerusalem, Ephrem, Epiphanius, Jerome. By A.D. 150, Mary's identification with Eve—creation's original woman—was established, and her portrayal is consistent in authors from diverse times and places: Rome, Palestine, Gaul, Asia Minor, North Africa, Syria, Cyprus, and Dalmatia.

The motif is, moreover, fully developed in the works of the earliest of those authors. They assume it as part of the apostolic faith. Justin Martyr is the first witness Newman calls on, quoting Justin's word to a Jewish interlocutor, Trypho, sometime in the 130s:

> [The Son of God] became man by the Virgin, in order that the disobedience which proceeded from the serpent might receive its destruction in the same manner in which it derived its origin. For Eve, who was a virgin and unde-filed, having conceived the word of the serpent, brought forth disobedience and death. But the Virgin Mary received faith and joy, when the angel Gabriel announced the good tidings to her that the Spirit of the Lord would come upon her, and the power of the Highest would over-shadow her: so that also the Holy Thing begotten of her is the Son of God; and she replied, "Let it be to me according to your word" [Luke 1:38].[1]

For Justin, God has reprised the act of creation by redeeming the world. And so the new creation bears many of the marks of the original. In each case, the woman is presented with a test, a choice. The first woman, Eve, chooses badly and sins against God, with catastrophic consequences for the human race. The second woman, Mary, chooses well and acquiesces to God's will, with saving consequences for the human race. In each case, Justin portrays the woman's action as decisive for subsequent history.

Irenaeus and Tertullian

In St. Irenaeus's writings, the idea is further developed as a work of "recapitulation." Irenaeus took the idea from St. Paul, who said that God's purpose was to "sum up all things" in Christ (Ephesians 1:10). Thus the story of Christ takes history and creation back to its origins. Writing just decades after Justin, Irenaeus explained:

> [God] has therefore, in his work of recapitulation, summed up all things, both waging war against our enemy, and crushing him who had at the beginning led us away captives in Adam.... He who should be born of a woman, [namely] from the Virgin, after the likeness of Adam, was preached as keeping watch for the head of the serpent.... For indeed the enemy would not have been fairly vanquished, unless it had been a man [born] of a woman who conquered him. For it was by means of a woman that he got the advantage over man at first, setting himself up as man's opponent.[2]

We see a primal man, a primal woman, and a serpent. It is the constellation of characters we have encountered in chapter three of the book of Genesis and chapter twelve of the book of Revelation. Jesus and Mary succeed where Adam and Eve failed.

Irenaeus returns to the New Eve motif repeatedly.[3] In one place, he describes Jesus as "the pure one, [who] purely opens the pure womb, which regenerates men in God."[4] Thus he indicates that Christians are in some sense born from the same womb as Jesus. He suggests a relationship between Mary and the Church that later Fathers work out in far greater detail. The regeneration in Christ, for Irenaeus, involves the mother. In the same chapter, he adds:

And how shall he (man) escape from the generation subject to death, if not by means of a new generation, given in a wonderful and unexpected manner (but as a sign of salvation) by God—that regeneration which flows from the virgin through faith?[5]

In a stunning passage, the Bishop of Lyons speaks poetically of Mary in terms that would inspire, more than a millennium later, devotion to the Virgin as "Undoer of Knots" or "Untier of Knots": "The knot of Eve's disobedience was loosed by the obedience of Mary. For what the virgin Eve had bound fast through unbelief, this did the virgin Mary set free through faith."[6]

The New Eve motif emerges also in the writings of Irenaeus's contemporary Tertullian.

It was by just the contrary operation that God recovered his own image and likeness, of which he had been robbed by the devil. For while Eve was yet a virgin, the ensnaring word had crept into her ear which was to build the edifice of death. Into a virgin's soul, in like manner, must be introduced that Word of God which was to raise the fabric of life; so that what had been reduced to ruin by this sex might by the same sex be recovered to salvation. As Eve had believed the serpent, so Mary believed the angel. The delinquency which the one occasioned by believing, the other by believing effaced.[7]

Elsewhere he compares Mary and Eve under the various titles and roles they share: *woman, virgin, betrothed*. He too hints at a maternal relationship between the New Eve and her offspring: "For if Eve means the mother of the living, behold, she is surnamed from a future circumstance!"[8]

Other Fathers

It is difficult to treat the New Eve motif in the space of a chapter. The material is too abundant, coming from many of the era's most honored voices: Cyprian, Athanasius, Ephrem, Ambrose.... Jerome reduced the motif to a lapidary phrase: "Death through Eve, life through Mary."[9] Prudentius wove it into elaborate hymns, whose imagery would become familiar in Christian art— and remains so to our own day.

> Thus sin in our parents sown
>   Brought forth ruin for the race;
> Good and evil having grown
>   From that primal root alone,
> Nought but death could guilt efface.
>
> But the Second Man behold
>   Come to re-create our kin:
> Not formed after common mould
>   But our God (O Love untold!)
> Made in flesh that knows not sin.
>
> Word of God incarnated,
>   By his awful power conceived,
> Whom a maiden yet unwed,
>   Innocent of marriage-bed,
> In her virgin womb received.
>
> Now we see the Serpent lewd
>   'Neath the woman's heel downtrod:
> Whence there sprang the deadly feud,
>   Strife for ages unsubdued,
> 'Twixt mankind and foe of God.

Yet God's mother, Maid adored,
　　Robbed sin's poison of its bane,
And the Snake, his green coils lowered,
　　Writhing on the sod, outpoured
Harmless now his venom's stain.[10]

What seems implicit in all the early Fathers is spelled out more clearly in the fourth century in the works of Epiphanius of Salamis (now the island of Cyprus). Epiphanius writes often of Mary as the New Eve, and he provides our earliest surviving text that identifies Mary with the book of Revelation's "woman clothed with the sun" (Revelation 12:1). He mentions the connection, in passing, in a discussion of the end of Mary's life.[11]

Epiphanius may also have been the first to apply the full meaning of Eve's name to Mary. The book of Genesis revealed that Adam "called his wife's name Eve, because she was the mother of all living" (Genesis 3:20). Epiphanius said the title better suited Mary than Eve.

> For Eve was called mother of the living…after the fall. It seems odd that she should receive such a grand title after having sinned…. Mary, on the contrary, truly introduced life itself into the world by giving birth to the Living One, so that Mary has become the Mother of the living.[12]

If Eve was the mother of fallen humanity—living but dying too— then Mary is the mother of *redeemed* humanity: those who are truly alive in Jesus Christ. She is the mother of other offspring, as the book of Revelation suggests (12:17)—the family of whom Jesus Christ is the "first-born among many brethren" (Romans 8:29).

The Church and the New Eve

Mary, then, is typically identified with the Church as she is typically identified with Eve. Mary is the fulfillment of Eve, the primal woman and mother, and Mary is the embodiment of the Christian Church.

The Fathers used the same symbols to describe Mary and the Church. Both are "mother"; both are "spouse"; both are "virgin"; both are embodiments of Jerusalem, Zion, and Israel. Both are the New Eve, Jacob's Ladder, the Ark of the Covenant.[13]

St. Ambrose writes: "Fittingly is she espoused, but virgin, because she prefigures the Church, which is undefiled yet wed."[14] St. Ephrem says, repeatedly and explicitly, "The Virgin Mary is a symbol of the Church."[15] It is from the Church's baptismal font that Christians are born to new life—born to Mother Church and born to Mary as her "other offspring."[16]

As Mother of All Living, Mary is "Mother of the Church"—a title that appears for the first time in an inscription from fifth-century Rome. It is on a tombstone for a boy named Macus, whose parents pray that "the Mother of the Church receive you on your return from this world."

More vivid are the intricate carvings on the ancient casket known as the "Trinity Sarcophagus" (or "Dogmatic Sarcophagus"). Its front depicts the creation of Adam and Eve above scenes from the life of Christ. Mary figures prominently, seated with the baby Jesus as they receive the Magi. One of the Magi points upward, toward the scene of the original creation, making the connection between the ancient type and its fulfillment.[17]

CHAPTER SEVEN

MOTHER OF GOD ※

WE CONSIDER COUNCILS OF THE CHURCH TO BE SOLEMN AFFAIRS. Their canons and decrees come down with authoritative weight and doctrinal freight. In icons, the ancient gatherings appear with timeless serenity—a cluster of identical men, uniformly bearded and haloed, gazing in the same direction. In reality, the ancient councils were more like brawls.

According to one account, at the first ecumenical council, at Nicaea in 325, St. Nicholas (yes, Santa Claus) punched the arch-heretic Arius, giving him a bloody nose. The Council of Chalcedon, in 451, was equal parts debate and gang fight. The patriarch of Constantinople was so battered from the pugilistic portions that he died from the injuries.

On a timeline, Ephesus falls between those two points, and it bears many of the same qualities as those better-known councils. In each, the bishops assembled to face a serious challenge to the Church's traditional doctrine about Jesus Christ. In each, they met the challenge with a wide range of human responses, from serious debate to subterfuge. The crisis before Ephesus was provoked by a man named Nestorius.

Defending Theotokos

A monk and priest in Syria, Nestorius won fame for his preaching and drew the attention of influential men in the imperial court.

In 428, the Emperor Theodosius II summoned him to the capital city, Constantinople, to serve as archbishop.

Nestorius was brilliant and had studied under the great theologian-bishop Theodore of Mopsuestia, so he arrived with a high degree of self-confidence. He could be pedantic and verbally fussy, and he was fond of the phrase "strictly speaking," which he used to punctuate his ever-finer semantic distinctions.

Arriving in the capital from Syria, he noted some significant differences in the way Christians expressed devotion. Constantinople, like Alexandria in Egypt, was known for its Marian fervor, which was all well and good—but Nestorius worried about his congregations' frequent invocation of Mary with the Greek term *Theotokos*, which means "God bearer" or "Mother of God."

"Strictly speaking," he noted, God can have no mother, since a mother must exist *before* the child she bears, and no one can pre-exist God. Nestorius didn't find the term *Theotokos* heretical (strictly speaking) but rather problematic and possibly misleading. So he actively discouraged its use and suggested *Christotokos* ("Christ bearer") as a suitable replacement.

And that was the beginning of his downfall. For he was pushing against the momentum of centuries of devotion practiced by multitudes of Christians—from the brightest intellectuals to common beggars. No one objected to the term *Christotokos*, which was undeniably true and orthodox. But they were unwilling to let go of the paradox—the indisputable facts standing in apparent contradiction—summarized in the word *Theotokos*. They were unwilling to throw over the powerful terms in which all their Christian ancestors had prayed.

The popular reaction was immediate and strong. Locals mocked their archbishop and wrote popular songs to satirize his prissiness. Some appealed to the bishops of the other major cities, begging them to intervene.

The patriarch of Alexandria—a man named Cyril—was happy to oblige. He had grown up with a deep devotion to the Blessed Virgin, fostered by his uncle and predecessor as bishop. He had also grown up with a peevish attitude toward the churches he viewed as rivals: Antioch and Constantinople. Nestorius, trained in Antioch and transferred to Constantinople—then arriving to dampen the Marian fervor of the congregations there—managed to push all of Cyril's buttons.

Cyril rose to the occasion by sending letters of inquiry to his colleague in Constantinople. He also enlisted the help of the pope in Rome. Still, Nestorius stood his ground, confident because he enjoyed the nearness and support of the emperor. He persuaded Theodosius, in fact, to call a council to settle the matter.

The emperor summoned the council to meet in the city of Ephesus—a city long associated with the life of the Virgin Mary. She had, according to tradition, lived there with the apostle John. By the time of the council, the city was home to one of the world's largest churches dedicated to the honor of the Blessed Virgin.

Nestorius had badly miscalculated in provoking the council. Cyril arrived with copious documentation of the Fathers' use of the term *Theotokos*, dating back two hundred years. Cyril's sermons and addresses at the council earned him the nickname "Seal of the Fathers." He invoked the witness of great theologians, from Origen and Athanasius to Basil and Gregory. He cited Scripture, including St. Elizabeth's use of the cognate term "mother of my

Lord" (Luke 1:43). He produced evidence from Tradition, and he reasoned from metaphysics. If Christians were to invoke Mary as "Mother of Christ"—but not also "Mother of God"—then they would so sunder the Son of God's two natures as to make them seem two different persons, one human and one divine.

Cyril articulated the theological principle in a positive way as the "communication of idioms" or "communication of properties": Whatever can be said about one of Christ's natures can be truthfully applied to his other nature. So Christians could truthfully say that God grew (see Luke 2:52), that God suffered, and even that God died, because the God-man experienced all these conditions, and he is one integrated person, truly human and truly divine. The principle is implied—and exemplified—in the writings of authors as early as Ignatius of Antioch (A.D. 107). It took a theologian of Cyril's genius to state it so clearly and succinctly.

Cyril prevailed at Ephesus.[1] The bishops overwhelmingly acclaimed the doctrine long hallowed by the worship of the Church: that Christ the God-man is a single subject, and so Mary could be called "Mother of God." She must not be called mother of his human nature alone, because mothers give birth not to a nature but to a person. The title "Mother of God" preserved the integrity of the incarnation of the eternal Word.

The bishops made it clear that they could not rule otherwise and remain faithful to the apostolic tradition. "We have been taught to hold these things by the holy Apostles and Evangelists, and all the God-inspired Scriptures, and in the true confessions of the blessed Fathers."[2]

Theologians won the day for the *Theotokos*. And throngs of common people celebrated the council's ruling by accompanying the bishops in a torchlight procession and singing hymns throughout the night.

Popular Devotion

Non-Catholic historians will sometimes speak as if the Council of Ephesus were the origin of the Church's Marian piety. But it wasn't. Ephesus provided the most complete articulation of a piety that had long been established in prayers and preaching.

Cyril's sequence of witnesses began with Origen, from the mid-third century. Cyril cited a book that, like most of Origen's work, has since been lost. From the same period, however, archeologists have recently recovered a papyrus in Egypt that includes a prayer to the Mother of God, the *Sub Tuum*. It is a prayer still widely in use today.

> We fly to your patronage,
> O holy Mother of God;
> despise not our petitions
> in our necessities,
> but deliver us always
> from all dangers,
> O glorious and blessed Virgin. Amen.[3]

Paleographers—experts in ancient handwriting—confidently date that scrap to A.D. 250. It is known as the John Rylands Papyrus 470, after the university library where it resides. It addresses Mary as *Theotokos* and asks directly for her help and intervention. It calls her holy, glorious, and blessed.

The prayer must have been extremely popular, because it survived in many ancient copies, in many places, in many languages: Greek, Latin, Syriac, Coptic, and Armenian. In the West it is best known by its first three words in Latin: *Sub Tuum Praesidium*.

The term *Theotokos* appears in all the great Alexandrian Fathers after Origen. St. Alexander employed it as he opposed the Arian heresy emerging in 319. As ever, Mary appears as the guarantor of a proper doctrine of Jesus Christ. Alexander wrote to the bishop of Constantinople (also named Alexander): "Our Lord Jesus Christ, in very deed and not merely in appearance, received a body from Mary Mother of God."[4] Alexander was an active and influential voice at the Council of Nicaea in 325, where even the emperor spoke of Mary as *Theotokos*.[5]

Alexander's successor, Athanasius, used the term often and in ways similar to his master's:

> Now the scope and character of Holy Scripture, as we have often said, is this: it contains a double account of the Savior; that he was ever God, and is the Son, being the Father's Word and Radiance and Wisdom; and that afterwards for us He took flesh of the Virgin Mary, Mother of God, and was made man.[6]

St. Cyril of Jerusalem used the term *Theotokos*, as did St. Ambrose of Milan. Prudentius phrased it poetically in many of his hymns, including his "Hymn on the Divinity of Christ":

> With his Mother's flesh God clothed himself,
> Since from Virginity he was made man.[7]

All of the great Cappadocian theologians use the term "Mother of God"—St. Basil, St. Gregory of Nazianzus, and St. Gregory of Nyssa—as do their lesser-known countrymen, such as Amphilochius. A full generation before the Council of Ephesus, Gregory of Nazianzus put the matter rather starkly: "If anyone does not believe that Holy Mary is the Mother of God, he is severed from the Godhead."[8]

Nor was the idea of Mary as "God bearer" alien to the Antiochene world, where Nestorius had received his education. Spurious letters attributed to Ignatius of Antioch, but composed there in the fourth century, refer to Mary as "her who bore the true God from her own womb."[9]

Outside Evidence

In the writings of the fourth century, there are many testimonies to the ubiquitous use of the term *Theotokos*. But perhaps the strangest testimony of all comes not from a Christian but an ex-Christian and vehement anti-Christian. It comes from Julian the Apostate, the emperor who led the charge, in the mid-fourth century, to re-paganize the Roman world.

Julian composed an anti-Christian tract called *Against the Galilaeans*, in which he tried to demonstrate the Bible's inconsistencies and the impossibility of Jesus's claims.

> "But," say the Galilaeans, "it agrees with the teachings of Isaiah. For Isaiah says, 'Behold the virgin shall conceive and bear a son'" (Isaiah 7:14). Now granted that this is said.... Does Isaiah anywhere say that a god will be born of the virgin? Then why do you not cease to call Mary the Mother of God, if Isaiah nowhere says that he who is born of the virgin is the "only begotten Son of God" (John 1:18) and "the firstborn of all creation" (Colossians 1:15)?...
>
> If, as you believe, the Word is God born of God and proceeded from the substance of the Father, why do you

say that the virgin is the mother of God? For how could she bear a god since she is, according to you, a human being?[10]

Julian anticipates the logic of Nestorius: If Mary did not precede God—so the argument goes—she could not ("strictly speaking") have mothered him.

What is most remarkable about Julian's argument is his observation that Christians habitually and ceaselessly called Mary "Mother of God." His witness is especially valuable since he had been raised a Christian and left the faith only in adulthood. His credibility rested on his status as a former insider. He would have gained nothing by exaggerating.

Julian noted the paradox of the title *Theotokos* and saw that it could not be resolved by rational means. He thought that this would arrive as news to the Christians. But Christians had noted it long before Julian was born, and they delighted in it. They sang it. They wrote it into poetry. They declared it to be indispensable.

P.S.

Let us consider a modern postscript to our ancient story.

One sad consequence of the Council of Ephesus was the schism that rent the Persian East from the Byzantine and Roman West. The division has lasted now for a millennium and a half.

There are those, no doubt, who would consider this division a "cold case," meriting no further attention. But Pope St. John Paul II chose to give it his close attention. He encouraged dialogue. And in 1994, he signed a "Common Christological Declaration" with Patriarch Mar Dinkha IV of the Church of the East. The document essentially resolved "the main dogmatic problem between the Catholic Church and the Assyrian Church."

In 2001, the Pontifical Council for Promoting Christian Unity went a step further and approved the sharing of Communion between the (Catholic) Chaldean Church and the (so-called Nestorian) Assyrian Church of the East. In the "Common Christological Declaration," both parties agreed:

> The humanity to which the Blessed Virgin Mary gave birth always was that of the Son of God himself. That is the reason why the Assyrian Church of the East is praying the Virgin Mary as "the Mother of Christ our God and Savior." In the light of this same faith the Catholic tradition addresses the Virgin Mary as "the Mother of God" and also as "the Mother of Christ." We both recognize the legitimacy and rightness of these expressions of the same faith and we both respect the preference of each Church in her liturgical life and piety.[11]

CHAPTER EIGHT

CONCEIVING HER CONCEPTION ✠

YOU CAN SEARCH THE SURVIVING WORKS OF THE FATHERS—AND all the apocrypha and all the graffiti in the catacombs—and you won't find a single instance of the phrase "Immaculate Conception" or its equivalent in Greek, Latin, Syriac, Coptic, or Armenian. It is a technical term developed by later theologians. We are, however, fully justified in searching for the reality described by the phrase.

Historians must do this when they read prescientific accounts of medical conditions. They examine the circumstances and symptoms, and then they draw a diagnostic conclusion using modern methods and vocabulary. Leukemia, for example, existed before 1827, but it was not named. Historians do not err—at least not necessarily—when they apply the term *leukemia* to a long-ago patient whose symptoms they have gleaned from many sources.

From what we find in the ancient sources, the early Christians seem to have observed a condition common to Jesus and Mary—a condition that made these two historical figures different from everyone else in history. They described it the best they could, in halting and cautious ways, sometimes erring in their "diagnosis." It fell to a later age to describe the condition with greater precision. It is not a *sickness* these ancestors in the faith were striving to describe but rather perfect health.

The New Adam

"The Lord, who knows his entire creation well, saw in it nothing like Mary."[1] So said a fourth-century author—quite likely St. Athanasius. While authorship of the text is uncertain, the ancients did not hesitate to assign the teaching to such an eminent authority of unquestionable orthodoxy.

In the entire creation, everything else was subject to the curse of the fall of Adam and Eve. When the first man and woman sinned, God pronounced their punishment in far-reaching terms.

> To the woman he said,
> "I will greatly multiply your pain in childbearing;
>> in pain you shall bring forth children,
> yet your desire shall be for your husband,
>> and he shall rule over you."
> And to Adam he said,
> "Because you have listened to the voice of your wife,
>> and have eaten of the tree
> of which I commanded you,
>> 'You shall not eat of it,'
> cursed is the ground because of you;
>> in toil you shall eat of it all the days of your life;
> thorns and thistles it shall bring forth to you;
>> and you shall eat the plants of the field.
> In the sweat of your face
>> you shall eat bread
> till you return to the ground,
>> for out of it you were taken;
> you are dust,
>> and to dust you shall return." (Genesis 3:16–19)

In the wake of the sin of Adam and Eve, everything was subject to entropy and decay. A life of pain and futility must end in corruption and dust. St. Paul wrote, "Death reigned...even over those whose sins were not like the transgression of Adam, who was a type of the one who was to come" (Romans 5:14).

If Adam was a "type," then he foreshadowed a fulfillment—a New Adam. Creation prefigured a new creation in Jesus Christ.

> For as in Adam all die, so also in Christ shall all be made alive....
>
> Thus it is written, "The first man Adam became a living soul"; the last Adam became a life-giving spirit.... The first man was from the earth, a man of dust; the second man is from heaven. (1 Corinthians 15:22, 45, 47)

In the redeeming work of the New Adam, God has said, "Behold, I make all things new" (Revelation 21:5).

Paul says explicitly that Jesus is the New Adam. The Fathers overwhelmingly—and from the earliest days of the Church—held that the Virgin Mary is the New Eve. Both conclusions are consequential for Christian doctrine and devotion.

First to Be Redeemed

From the first generation, Christians insisted that Mary did not suffer labor pains in giving birth. We have seen this already in the *Ascension of Isaiah*, the *Odes of Solomon*, *The Infancy Gospel of James*, and other early texts (see chapter 3). Why did this matter so much to them?

It mattered because they believed that the new creation was a reprise of the old. They believed that God had made the conditions of the new creation to be recognizably like the conditions of the original creation. The Gospel story, like the Genesis story, revolves around the interaction of a man, a woman, and a serpent.

It is reasonable to expect that the New Man and New Woman should enjoy the privileges of their first forebears. So as the early Christians told the story, Mary's pregnancy and birth proceeded without pain, as if God had never pronounced the punishing curse of Genesis 3:16. The message of the miraculous birth is that Mary did not merit the punishment. Like Eve before the sin, she was sinless and virginal. The physical effects of sin apparently did not apply to Mary.

This led the Fathers, hesitantly, to the conclusion that Mary was without sin. They hesitated because they wanted to preserve the "normality" of her motherhood. They did not want to give aid and comfort to heretics who wished to deny Jesus's true humanity. Still, they made bold statements. Listen to Ephrem of Syria as he sings to Jesus:

> You alone and your Mother
>   are more beautiful than any others,
> for there is no blemish in you
>   nor any stains upon your Mother.
> Who of my children
>   can compare in beauty to these?[2]

St. Ambrose called Mary "a Virgin not only undefiled but a Virgin whom grace had made inviolate, free of every stain of sin."[3]

In the second-century epitaph of the bishop St. Abercius, the Virgin is hailed as "spotless" and "immaculate." In the third century, St. Hippolytus said that Christ "was without sin, made of imperishable wood, as regards his humanity; that is, of the virgin and the Holy Ghost inwardly, and outwardly of the word of God, like an ark overlaid with purest gold."[4]

St. Augustine, who was unsparingly realistic about the human capacity for sin, would not even allow himself to speak of the Virgin Mary in the context of his discussion of sin. He acknowledges that all have sinned but goes on to say:

> We must except the holy Virgin Mary, concerning whom I wish to raise no question when it touches the subject of sins, out of honor to the Lord; for from him we know what abundance of grace for overcoming sin in every particular was conferred upon her who had the merit to conceive and bear him who undoubtedly had no sin. [5]

Mary's singular merit was itself a gift from the Lord. St. Ephrem sang to Jesus:

> You, who are your mother's beauty, yourself adorned her
> with everything!
> She was, by her nature, your bride already before you
> came.[6]

In the first movement of his saving work, Jesus redeemed his mother. She was, said St. Ambrose, the first to be saved: "It is not to be wondered at that when the Lord was about to redeem the world, he began his work from Mary, so that she, through whom salvation was being prepared for all, should be the first to draw salvation from her Son."[7] She was, said St. Gregory of Nazianzus, "first in body and soul purified by the Holy Spirit."[8]

Mary's Gift

In the modern age, in the West, we have tended to think of Mary's special condition in negative terms. She is "conceived *without sin.*" She is spot*less*. She is *im*maculate. We speak as if a lack of sin somehow indicates a deficit of something.

The early Christians, however, tended to express the same truth in positive terms. The ancient liturgies refer to Mary as *Panagia*— Greek for "All-Holy."[9] This is the devotional consequence of the Fathers' reading of Luke 1:28, the angel Gabriel's greeting to Mary: "Hail, full of grace!" To be *full* of grace is to be empty of sin. It is not a deficit but a superabundance.

A vessel full of grace has no capacity—no room—for sin. St. Augustine said, "An abundance of grace was conferred on her, who merited to conceive and bear him whom we know was without sin."[10]

Mary's gift was singular. St. Ephrem wrote that Moses was illumined temporarily when he saw God (see Exodus 34:29–30), but Mary's light was interior and permanent.[11]

The New Testament shows no evidence that Mary ever sinned— which is unusual for a major character in the Gospels. On the other hand, it shows ample evidence of her virtue—the overflow of a soul "full of grace." Thus St. Ambrose asked, "What is greater than the Mother of God?"

> What more glorious than she whom Glory itself chose? What more chaste than she who bore a body without contact with another body? For why should I speak of her other virtues? She was a virgin not only in body but also in mind, who stained the sincerity of its disposition by no guile, who was humble in heart, grave in speech, prudent in mind, sparing of words, studious in reading, resting her hope not on uncertain riches, but on the prayer of the poor, intent on work, modest in discourse; wont to seek

not man but God as the judge of her thoughts, to injure no one, to have goodwill towards all, to rise up before her elders, not to envy her equals, to avoid boastfulness, to follow reason, to love virtue. When did she pain her parents even by a look? When did she disagree with her neighbors? When did she despise the lowly? When did she avoid the needy?[12]

Most Holy Lady

In thinking about the mystery of Mary's sinlessness, many of the Fathers felt an almost Marian perplexity: "How can this be?" (Luke 1:34). They found the conclusion to be inevitable but struggled to square it with other scriptural texts (for example, Romans 3:12, 23). Some felt constrained to read between the lines of the Gospels to find a sin for Mary! Some of the greatest—Origen, St. Basil the Great, and St. John Chrysostom—erred badly in their speculation about Mary's condition regarding sin and grace.

The Church's teaching authority did not definitively rule on the matter until 1854, when Pope Blessed Pius IX, after consulting with the bishops and faithful throughout the world, solemnly defined the doctrine of Mary's Immaculate Conception. In the constitution *Ineffabilis Deus*, he pronounced that the Blessed Virgin "in the first instance of her conception, by a singular privilege and grace granted by God, in view of the merits of Jesus Christ, the Savior of the human race, was preserved exempt from all stain of original sin."

In this, Mary was like the first woman, Eve. But unlike Eve, she retained the gift. She never sinned. There is a beautiful and necessary symmetry here between the type and its fulfillment. St. Augustine said:

Our Lord...was not averse to males, for he took the form of a male, nor to females, for of a female he was born. Besides, there is a great mystery here: that just as death comes to us through a woman, Life is born to us through a woman; that the devil, defeated, would be tormented by each nature, feminine and masculine, as he had taken delight in the defection of both.[13]

An anonymous Syriac hymn of the ancient Church expresses delight in the circumstance: A woman is called, as Prudentius would say, to crush the head of the snake.

From among those below it was not a male
who was appointed to repay the debt,
but a female, one chosen from among women.
She listened, spoke and established something quite new,
thus gaining renown in the world.[14]

It was another Syriac-speaking father, St. Ephrem in the fourth century, who sang her renown in the most exalted language:

Most holy Lady, Mother of God, alone most pure in soul and body, alone exceeding all perfection of purity..., alone made in your entirety the home of all the graces of the Most Holy Spirit, and hence exceeding beyond all compare even the angelic virtues in purity and sanctity of soul and body....

My Lady most holy,...all-pure, all-immaculate, all-stainless, all-undefiled, all-incorrupt, all-inviolate,...spotless robe of him who clothes himself with light as with a garment,...flower unfading,...purple woven by God, alone most immaculate.[15]

Theology, like medicine, is a progressive science. Each generation builds upon the work of generations gone before. Terms change, but the realities they describe remain constant. If the ancient Fathers never mentioned the "Immaculate Conception," they surely knew it nonetheless, and they surely spoke of it.

CHAPTER NINE

ASSUMING HER ASSUMPTION ✠

IN 1950, POPE PIUS XII MADE HEADLINES WHEN HE PROCLAIMED the Virgin Mary's Assumption to be revealed dogma, which Christians are bound in faith to believe. At the end of his Apostolic Constitution *Munificentissimus Deus*, he wrote:

> By the authority of our Lord Jesus Christ, of the Blessed Apostles Peter and Paul, and by our own authority, we pronounce, declare, and define it to be a divinely revealed dogma: that the Immaculate Mother of God, the ever Virgin Mary, having completed the course of her earthly life, was assumed body and soul into heavenly glory.[1]

Earlier in the document, he cited testimonies from Tradition, liturgy, and the saints, including some from the patristic era. He summarized the theological argument in a single sentence:

> She, by an entirely unique privilege, completely overcame sin by her Immaculate Conception, and as a result she was not subject to the law of remaining in the corruption of the grave, and she did not have to wait until the end of time for the redemption of her body.[2]

The reaction from Protestant quarters was swift and furious. The American Lutheran theologian Reinhold Niebuhr raged against the pope's action in an essay titled "The Increasing Isolation of the Catholic Church," which appeared in the magazine *Christianity and Crisis*.[3] The dogma, he thundered, "incorporates a legend of the Middle Ages into the official teachings of the Church, thereby placing the final capstone on the Mariolatry of the Roman Church."

And that was a guarded moment. To his friend and colleague Paul Tillich, Niebuhr referred to the dogma as "a slap in the face of the whole modern world."[4] Tillich agreed with him.

The Oxford don and Anglican churchman R.L.P Milburn accused the pope of making "fantasy, however pious, to masquerade as fact." He dismissed Mary's Assumption as nothing more than "Coptic romance."[5]

This backlash came not from the fringes but from the mainstream of the Protestant academy. Niebuhr and Tillich were teaching at New York's Union Theological Seminary. Milburn's comments are embedded in his 1952 Bampton Lectures at Oxford—then the most distinguished lectureship in Protestant theology. The consensus of these Protestant scholars was that Catholic piety had led the pope to willfully disregard the evidence of history.

But history itself is a master of irony, and more recent historians are calling into question the anti-Marian bias of the dogma's critics—and concluding that the traditions of Mary's Assumption reach back much further than men like Niebuhr and Milburn were willing to allow.

Tracing Tradition

The case of the Assumption is somewhat like that of the Immaculate Conception—though in the case of the Assumption, the particular terminology did emerge in the time of the Fathers. The early traditions refer to the end of Mary's life as her *dormition*—that is, her "falling asleep"—or her *assumption*, meaning her transport to heaven. The terms are not exclusive. They describe two discrete movements in a single event.

That event, however—like the notion of Mary's Immaculate Conception—is not so much expounded in the early Fathers but seems rather to be assumed, implied, and put forward in a cautious or hesitant way. Still, it is undeniably there. The evangelical Protestant biblical scholar Richard Bauckham traces the tradition to "the fourth century at the latest, but perhaps considerably earlier."[6]

The scholar, however, who has done the most to rehabilitate the Assumption tradition in the secular academy is Stephen J. Shoemaker of the University of Oregon. Shoemaker has produced not only an extensive study of the subject (more than five hundred pages)[7] but also annotated translations of all the relevant ancient texts—from originals in Greek, Syriac, Ethiopic, Latin, and Coptic. He concludes in a recent paper:

> Marian piety did not suddenly burst onto the scene in Constantinople during the late 420s through some kind of spontaneous generation, as it sometimes can be made to appear. The early Dormition apocrypha disclose the existence of Marian intercession and even Marian cult well before the Council of Ephesus.[8]

The first author to deal with the Assumption explicitly was St. Epiphanius, writing in the late fourth century. He speaks of it twice, in fact, and together these passages tell us much about the status of the idea in his time.

In the earlier of the two texts, Epiphanius declares that we do not know with certainty what happened at the end of Mary's earthly days. He presents several hypotheses but favors none.

> Most assuredly, if the Holy Virgin died and was buried, her rest is in honor, her end in purity, her crown in virginity. Or, again, supposing she was put to death, according to what is written: *Her soul, too, a sword shall pierce*—then her glory is amongst the martyrs, and her holy body is blessed, since through her it was that light arose upon the world. Or, on the other hand, [perhaps] she remained— since God is able to do whatever he wills—and, in fact, no one knew her end....
>
> The saints are in honor, and their repose in glory, their departure from this life in perfection, their lot in bliss, their choir with that of angels in holy mansions, their habitation in heaven.[9]

Epiphanius makes it clear that there are many perfectly orthodox ways of approaching the question of Mary's earthly end. The Church, at that time, had not spoken dogmatically on the subject. However, later in the same work—which was probably compiled over the course of many years—Epiphanius offers his own opinion. In a discussion of the honor that Christians owe to Mary, he says, "And if I should say anything more in her praise, she is like Elijah, who was a virgin from his mother's womb, he remained so perpetually, and was assumed and has not seen death."[10]

Epiphanius seems to be familiar with the traditions preserved in a widely circulated text known as the *Six Books* (translated into English as *The Departure of My Lady Mary from This World*).

Shoemaker, Bauckham, and others have identified these as the earliest traditions to be preserved.

The account in the *Six Books* purports to tell of Mary's last days. The apostles are summoned from around the world to witness Mary's passing—Peter from Rome, John from Ephesus, Thomas from India, Paul from Tiberias. Philip is even raised from the grave. They are miraculously transported to Mary's home in Bethlehem, where they see her taken away in a heavenly chariot, reminding the onlookers of the Old Testament departure of the prophet Elijah.

Moses and Elijah

Mary was not, after all, the first person to be assumed into heaven. The Jews honored the memory of at least two historical figures who—according to tradition—had been taken up to heaven at the end of their earthly lives.[11]

The prophet Elijah was speaking with his disciple Elisha. "And as they still went on and talked, behold, a chariot of fire and horses of fire separated the two of them. And Elijah went up by a whirlwind into heaven" (2 Kings 2:11). We read also in the first book of Maccabees: "Elijah because of great zeal for the law was taken up into heaven" (2:58). He was bodily assumed.

Long before Elijah, however, was Moses. An apocryphal text called the *Assumption of Moses* (composed slightly before the time of Christ) tells of the Lawgiver's long farewell address to his successor, Joshua. The book proceeds to tell of a dispute between the devil and the archangel Michael over the disposition of Moses's body. The dispute is noteworthy because it appears in the New Testament Letter of St. Jude (1:9). And the text is relevant to our discussion because Moses's body eventually found its way past the devil and into heaven.

Moses and Elijah are both able to appear with Jesus at his transfiguration on Mount Tabor: "And behold, there appeared to them Moses and Elijah, talking with him" (Matthew 17:3). Both men are alive, they are embodied, and they can be seen and heard.

They are, curiously enough, two Old Testament figures often associated with the Blessed Virgin Mary. As we saw earlier in this chapter, both Epiphanius and the *Six Books* draw the comparison between Mary's assumption and Elijah's. Other Fathers too bring up either Moses or Elijah (or both) when discussing Mary. St. Ephrem does it often.

In one of his hymns on the nativity, he tells the story of Elijah's disappearance:

> For Elijah they went and searched the mountains (2 Kings 2:16): as they sought him on earth, they the more confirmed that he was taken up. Their searching bore witness that he was taken up, in that it found him not.
>
> If then prophets that had had forewarning of Elijah's ascension, doubted as it were of his going up, how much more would impure men speak slander of the Son? By their own guards he convinced them that he was risen again.

And then Ephrem abruptly changes the subject—with no transition—to the Virgin Mary.

> To your mother, Lord, no man knew what name to give. Should he call her Virgin, her Child stood [there]; and married no man knew her to be! If then none comprehended your mother, who shall suffice for you? [12]

We cannot know whether Ephrem intended to make the association—the assumed prophet and the assumed virgin—but it does seem likely.

Other Syriac hymn writers evoke the Elijah story, speaking of Mary herself as a "chariot of flesh" who bore the fiery Messiah.

A chariot of flesh did Mary become,
enabling her to escort the Fiery One in her bosom.
The angel stood amazed at the daughter of humanity
as she carried the Lord of all humanity.[13]

The poet known as Simon the Potter wrote:

Come in peace, O chariot of flesh
that carries him who carries all.[14]

Ephrem taught that Moses and Elijah were able to ascend to heaven because of the chastity with which they lived their earthly lives:

Because Elijah restrained the desire of the body, he with-held rain from the adulterous; because he kept under his body, he withheld dew from the whoremongers, who let their fountains be loosely poured out.

Because the hidden fire of the lust of the body ruled not in him, to him the fire from on high was obedient. And since he subdued on the earth the lust of the flesh, he went up there where holiness dwells and is at peace....

Moses, who divided and separated himself from his wife, divided the sea....[15]

What was true of the pure men Moses and Elijah should be all the more true for the woman known to history as "the Virgin."

Indeed, the Lawgiver and the prophet merely "longed for" the Messiah; Mary bore him in her womb.

> For him Elijah longed, and when he saw him not on earth, he, through faith most thoroughly cleansed, mounted up in heaven to see him. Moses saw him and Elijah; the meek man from the depth ascended, the zealous from on high descended, and in the midst beheld the Son. They symbolized the mystery of his Advent.[16]

As at the dawn of his Advent, so at the end of Mary's days in Bethlehem, the angel Gabriel appeared to her. (So we read in the *Six Books*.) He addresses her as "Mother of God."

> Be strong and do not fear, O Theotokos! Arise and go to Bethlehem, and remain there until you see armies of angels, the apostles, and every creature coming to you to pray to you and proclaim you blessed.[17]

CHAPTER TEN

STAR OF EVANGELIZATION ✠

IN RECENT YEARS, THE POPES HAVE HERALDED MARY AS THE "STAR of the New Evangelization."[1] It is good for us to recall that she was the star of the first evangelization as well—and it is good for us to know how well the first succeeded.

At the Council of Ephesus, St. Cyril of Alexandria surveyed the Church's progress since the apostolic age, and he gave ample credit to the Blessed Virgin.

> We salute you, for in your holy womb was confined him who is beyond all limitation. Because of you the Holy Trinity is glorified and adored,… the fallen race of man is taken up on high; all creatures possessed by the madness of idolatry have attained knowledge of the truth; believers receive holy baptism; the oil of gladness is poured out; the Church is established throughout the world; pagans are brought to repentance.
>
> What more is there to say? Because of you the light of the only-begotten Son of God has shone upon those who sat in darkness and in the shadow of death; prophets pronounced the word of God; the apostles preached salvation to the Gentiles; the dead are raised to life, and kings rule by the power of the Holy Trinity.[2]

The first evangelization began with the opening scenes in the Acts of the Apostles, where Mary sat with the Church, awaiting the Holy Spirit. The period culminated, we might say, with the Peace of Constantine, following the emperor's decrees of toleration issued in 313 and afterward. Through those first three centuries, the practice of the faith was illegal—a capital crime—and was intermittently persecuted. Yet the Church grew worldwide at a steady rate of 40 percent per decade.[3] At the time of the last persecution, Christians likely made up the majority of the population in many cities.

From the eve of Pentecost onward, Mary was present with the apostles and their successors in their astonishing work of proclamation and conversion. She is most directly associated with the apostle John, to whom Jesus entrusted her from the cross (see John 19:26–27). According to tradition, she accompanied John to Ephesus, the seat of his authority as he governed the Church in Asia Minor. In some accounts, she returned to Palestine to end her days.

In the *Six Books*, as we have seen, all of the apostles, as well as the evangelists and other New Testament figures, are summoned to Mary's side as she closes the earthly portion of her life. Some of the later renditions have Thomas arriving too late from faraway India, but Mary appears to him and leaves him with a token of her appreciation, a *cincture* or binding garment.

The story of Thomas is striking, because he receives *visible* help: Mary *appears* to him. He receives what came to be called the grace of an *apparition*. His was not to be the last reported appearance of the Blessed Virgin.

The most famous might be the vision of John the seer in the book of Revelation, chapter twelve. But again, reputable scholars differ on whether the woman in that scene should be interpreted as the Virgin Mary—and even whether the chapter reports a true sensory experience or is merely conforming to certain literary conventions of Jewish and Christian antiquity.[4] In any case, many other Marian apparitions followed. The Church continued to fly to her patronage and ask her intercession—and receive her help.

Star of Wonder

St. Gregory of Pontus is known to history as the Wonderworker. He was born into a pagan family in Cappadocia, Asia Minor. He converted to Christianity as a teenager, and in his youth he traveled to the Holy Land to study with the renowned Scripture scholar Origen. Gregory's call, however, was to be a missionary, an evangelizer, and so he returned to his home country, a land that was overwhelmingly pagan.

Cappadocia ranged from the Taurus Mountains to the Black Sea—land that is today part of Turkey. When Gregory first became its bishop, according to his own account, there were only seventeen Christians in the area's capital city. After thirteen years of his preaching, however, there were only seventeen pagans left in the city!

His life is well attested. Anecdotes appear in the works of the Cappadocian bishops who were his successors. One detailed witness is interesting to us here because of the event that appears to be the turning point in his ministry. The story comes to us in a *panegyric*, a speech of praise and tribute, written in A.D. 380 by St. Gregory of Nyssa, who had been named for the Wonderworker.[5] One of the sources for the younger Gregory's stories was his own grandmother, Macrina, who had been an eyewitness to the Wonderworker's ministry.

Shortly after arriving back in Cappadocia, Gregory of Pontus was troubled because the Christian flock there—tiny as it was— suffered terrible divisions. Their disagreements ran deep, touching upon the core doctrines of the Trinity and the Lord's incarnation. The situation left him sleepless.

One night while he was at prayer, two figures appeared to him—a dignified old man and a beautiful young woman. Both were radiant with a light so strong that Gregory had to avert his eyes. As the vision continued, Gregory learned that the old man was the apostle John and the woman was the Blessed Virgin. Together they instructed the young bishop in the Christian doctrine he was to pass on to the people of Cappadocia. At the heart of the vision was the revelation of a creed that Gregory would use as he instructed converts for baptism.

The Wonderworker's vision, we are told, filled Gregory with confidence, and "like an athlete," he rushed to the city to begin his work of building the Church. Within thirteen years, he had overcome not only the divisions in his little flock but also the idolatry and demon worship of the local pagan populace.

The Cappadocian Church would forever bear the mark of the apparition Gregory received. In the fourth century, Gregory's successors—known to history as the Cappadocian Fathers— emerged as the great defenders of the traditional doctrines of the Trinity and the Incarnation. With clarity, precision, and rigor, they battled Arianism and its descendant heresies, and they prevailed. Their theology, which began with the creed of Gregory, became the touchstone of orthodoxy in the centuries after the Council of Nicaea—the definitive interpretation of the council's doctrine.

Path of Pilgrims

As a theologian and preacher, Theophilus of Alexandria occupies an important place among the Copts in Egypt. Patriarch of Alexandria from 384 to 412, his deeds are well attested. In the West, he is best known for his bitter opposition (alas) to St. John Chrysostom. Theophilus was the third to hold the patriarchate after St. Athanasius, and he was the uncle to his most famous successor, St. Cyril.

Among his own people, Theophilus is remembered for his Marian piety. He was famous for naming churches after Mary. On his way to the dedication of one of them, he reportedly had a vision in which the Blessed Virgin revealed to him the Holy Family's route as they fled Herod's persecution. On the strength of this vision, Theophilus confirmed the traditional shrines of Christian Egypt.

The oldest surviving record of this apparition is an account in Sahidic Coptic, titled as a sermon by Theophilus himself.[6] The fragment is from the first millennium, but it is difficult to date with greater precision. The sermon is interesting because it plots the Holy Family's flight into Egypt as a rather exact correspondence to the apocalyptic vision of Revelation 12. The woman and child, persecuted by the dragon, take refuge in the mountains of Egypt. Pilgrims gathered there in the fourth century—and still do today.

The vision of Theophilus occurs at a much different stage of evangelization than that of Gregory. Egypt was mostly Christian by that time, and the Emperor Theodosius was busy eradicating, by brute force, the last remnants of the old pagan religion. It is likely that the Marian shrines of Egypt—with their pilgrimages and miracles, attested to even in the first millennium—had a salutary effect on the subsequent life of the Church.

Blessed Lady

The reports of Mary's appearances to Theophilus and Gregory—and to Thomas and John—seem anomalous in the history of apparitions. In later centuries, she most often appeared not to hierarchs but to children. We find such a story in the works of yet another Gregory, the first pope by that name, who reigned from 590 to 604. Gregory lived many decades after our end point, the Council of Ephesus, but he is the figure who most effectively conserved the Christian legacy—the teachings of the Fathers—for the generations to come.

In his *Dialogues*, Gregory tells the story of a young girl named Musa who received two visits from the Virgin, whom she addressed as "Blessed Lady." His source for the story was Probus, who was still alive, well known, and respected as the abbot of a monastery in Rome.[7] Musa's story is significant because it led to the young girl's repentance and reform. Her transformation was immediately noticeable to all her family members—some of whom were still alive, at Gregory's writing, to tell the tale.

As in modern times, so in ancient: Marian apparitions are a harbinger not only of doctrinal renewal but also of moral reform. As private revelations, they transform a soul, who transforms many souls.

As Christians first evangelized the world—and met with remarkable success—they looked to Mary, and sometimes they saw her. And then they succeeded all the more. So the popes bid us today to look to the Star of the New Evangelization.

CHAPTER ELEVEN

THE ILLUMINATED GOSPELS ☀

RABULLA WAS A SCRIBE AT A REMOTE SYRIAN MONASTERY IN THE sixth century. We know nothing more about him than his name and the fact that he produced one of the masterworks of art history. We know him because he signed his work, an edition of the four Gospels in their Syriac translation.

The Rabulla Gospels are among the oldest illustrated New Testament books to survive to the modern age.[1] They differ in style, but not so much in content, from the still older (perhaps fourth-century) Abuna Garima Gospels, a treasure of early Ethiopian Christianity and monument of the Ge'ez language. These ancient Bibles are remarkable for their Marian art. Rabulla (if indeed he was the illustrator as well as the scribe) served art as St. Cyril of Alexandria served the science of theology. He too was a "Seal of the Fathers." He gave visual expression to the piety of his spiritual ancestors. And what does he show us?

In the Rabulla Gospels, we see Mary at the heart of the Church. At the Ascension, she dominates the earthly scene. As her son rises, attended by angels and seraphim, she stands upon the ground with her arms outstretched, surrounded by the apostles. The apostles look fearfully to the sky, while Mary gazes at the reader. She appears to be exempt from the angelic reprimand.

And while they were gazing into heaven as he went, behold, two men stood by them in white robes, and said, "Men of Galilee, why do you stand looking into heaven? This Jesus, who was taken up from you into heaven, will come in the same way as you saw him go into heaven." (Acts 1:10–11)

Mary's expression shows serene faith in the midst of a troubled Church, uncertain of its future.

The illustration of Pentecost is similarly composed. Mary stands at the center of the apostles as they all together receive the Holy Spirit, depicted as a dove and as fire.

All these with one accord devoted themselves to prayer, together with the women and Mary the mother of Jesus....

When the day of Pentecost had come, they were all together in one place. And suddenly a sound came from heaven like the rush of a mighty wind, and it filled all the house where they were sitting. And there appeared to them tongues as of fire, distributed and resting on each one of them. And they were all filled with the Holy Spirit. (Acts 1:14; 2:1–4)

Now fortified by the divine Gift, the disciples, with Mary, look directly at the reader. Their hands are raised as if to give a blessing, but her hand is held highest. She is the preeminent disciple of Jesus Christ. Faith gives her confidence. Hope keeps her eyes trained forward, fixed on her task. Love leads her to give herself fully as a benediction to others.

In yet another illumination of the Rabulla Gospels, Mary appears holding the infant Jesus. Both seem to gaze at the reader, who gazes back. Such is Mary as she appeared to the early Christians. Such is Mary as she appeared in the early Church.

Mary in the Church

Mary always stands in the midst of that Church. That is what we learn from the constant witness of the Fathers.

She is in its Scriptures.

She is in its preaching and proclamation.

She is in its poetry and songs.

She is in its creeds.

She is in the catacombs in Rome and the cemeteries of the Fayoum.

She is in its mosaics, frescos, and sculpture.

She is in graffiti at the Church's pilgrim shrines.

She is in the apocrypha and *pseudepigrapha*.

She is in the Church's calendar, on her feasts and those of her son.

She is burnished onto oil lamps and minted in coins.

She is ever among her fellow disciples. She is a mother to them, because she mothers her son, in whom they live.

Who testifies to the life of Mary in the Church? In the chapters of this book, we have heard from great intellectuals and emperors. We have heard as well the shouts of a common urban crowd. We have heard from high culture and low. And make no mistake—as Jesus has been loved in misguided and tasteless ways, so has Mary.

An ancient book recently discovered in Egypt is *The Gospel of the Lots of Mary*.[2] It has been described as the Magic Eight Ball of the ancient world. Presented as an aid to divining the future, it contains thirty-seven "oracles"—vague but portentous statements that could be applied to any circumstance and interpreted in various ways. For example: "Do you not remember what has happened to you before today?"

Mary does not figure in the oracles. She seems to be on the title page only for marketing purposes. But that, in itself, witnesses to her great popularity, even so far out at the fringes of devotion.

Mary figures also in the so-called "magical papyri" found in the Egyptian desert.[3] Jesus's name is similarly misused in the papyri. Superstition is the tribute credulity pays to true faith.

While many ancient songs that honor Mary are of sublime quality—as we have seen in works of Ephrem and Prudentius—others are exemplars of mediocrity. One twentieth-century compiler of Marian hymns has remarked on the survival of songs that have "neither literary nor esthetic value."[4] Yet they survived for us to study because, in spite of their poor quality, there were many copies in circulation. Christians, then as now, love to "sing of Mary."

Hyperdulia

The honor given to Mary was different—in degree and in kind—from the honor given to her Son. St. Epiphanius made this point in the fourth century as he railed against the Collyridian sect, which went so far as to offer idolatrous sacrifice to the Virgin. St. John of Damascus elaborated with greater precision at the very end of the patristic era.[5] *Latria* (adoration) belongs only to God. *Dulia* is the honor we give to deserving people—similar to the respect we owe our parents and rulers.

Tradition has come to speak of the special honor given to Mary as *hyperdulia*—a heightened form of veneration. We have seen it consistently in the works of the Fathers: "The Lord, who knows his entire creation well, saw in it nothing like Mary."[6]

O noble Virgin, truly you are greater than any other greatness. For who is your equal in greatness, O dwelling place of God the Word? To whom among all creatures shall I compare you, O Virgin? You are greater than them all.[7]

St. Amphilochius called out to her in a singular way:

O Mary, O Mary,... O humanity who became the bodily substance of the Word and for that reason became more honorable than the spiritual virtues of heaven!...

Where now is that hostile and bewildered dragon? Where is that cursed and execrable dragon, who had claimed that his throne would be raised to the heights of heaven?[8]

Devotion to Mary was, for the early Christians, the hinge of the doctrine of Jesus. For St. Ignatius, it was a proof equally effective against those who denied Jesus's humanity and those who denied his divinity. Athanasius—called "the Father of Orthodoxy"—invoked her in the same way. So did Cyril, the "Seal of the Fathers."

Mary is the hinge of doctrine because she is the hinge of history. God awaited her yes at the pivotal moment. Thus, St. Irenaeus in the second century called her the "cause of salvation, both to herself and the whole human race."[9] She was not the Savior, but she was indeed the "cause of salvation" and the first to be saved.

Mary's place in history, doctrine, and devotion is extraordinary, exceptional, unique. Her vocation was distinctive and singular, and she responded with unfailing fidelity. In their turn, the Fathers gave her a singular devotion—Athanasius called it "commemoration"[10]—that developed over the centuries, expressing itself in countless ways.

The devotion, they believed, would have its reward when all types found their fulfillment. St. Jerome marveled at this.

> What will be the glory of that day when Mary, the mother of the Lord, shall come to meet you, accompanied by her virgin choirs! When, the Red Sea past and Pharaoh drowned with his host, Miriam, Aaron's sister, her timbrel in her hand, shall chant to the answering women: "Sing to the Lord, for he has triumphed gloriously" (Exodus 15:20–21).[11]

John Henry Newman, "The Dignity of Mary" ☒

We have no witness from before the fourth century who identifies Mary with the "woman clothed with the sun" in the book of Revelation. The doctrine of the Fathers does not require it, but the Fathers do seem to assume it as background—in discussing Mary as the New Eve, her assumption, and so on.

One of the greatest patristic scholars in modern times, Blessed Cardinal John Henry Newman, a convert to Catholicism, argued persuasively for the connection. The following excerpt is from his letter to a Protestant colleague, E.B. Pusey. A more modern version appears in *The Mystical Rose*, an anthology of Newman's Marian writings.

Here let us suppose that our first parents had overcome in their trial; and had gained for their descendants for ever the full possession, as if by right, of the privileges which were promised to their obedience—grace here and glory hereafter. Is it possible that those descendants, pious and happy from age to age in their temporal homes, would have forgotten their benefactors? Would they not have followed them in thought into the heavens, and gratefully commemorated them on earth? The history of the temptation, the craft of the serpent, their steadfastness in obedience—the loyal vigilance, the sensitive purity of Eve—the great issue, salvation wrought out for all generations—would have been never from their minds, ever welcome to their ears. This would have taken place from the necessity of our nature.

Every nation has its mythical hymns and epics about its first fathers and its heroes. The great deeds of Charlemagne, Alfred, Coeur de Lion, Louis the ninth, Wallace, Joan of Arc, do not die; and though their persons are gone from us, we make much of their names. Milton's Adam, after his fall, understands the force of this law and shrinks from the prospect of its operation.

> Who of all ages to succeed, but, feeling
> The evil on him brought by me, will curse
> My head? Ill fare our ancestor impure,
> For this we may thank Adam.

If this anticipation of the first man has not been fulfilled in the event, it is owing to the exigencies of our penal life, our state of perpetual change, and the ignorance and unbelief incurred by the fall; also because, fallen as we are, still from the hopefulness of our nature, we feel more pride in our national great men, than dejection at our national misfortunes. Much more then in the great kingdom and people of God—the Saints are ever in our sight, and not as mere ineffectual ghosts or dim memories, but as if present bodily in their past selves. It is said of them, "Their works do follow them"; what they were here, such are they in heaven and in the Church. As we call them by their earthly names, so we contemplate them in their earthly characters and histories. Their acts, callings, and relations below, are types and anticipations of their present mission above.

Even in the case of our Lord Himself, whose native home is the eternal heavens, it is said of Him in His state of glory, that He is "a Priest for ever"; and when He comes again, He will be recognized by those who pierced Him, as being the very same that He was on earth. The only question is, whether the Blessed Virgin had a part, a real part, in the economy of grace, whether, when she was on earth, she secured by her deeds any claim on our memories; for, if she did, it is impossible we should put her away from us, merely because she is gone hence, and should not look at her still according to the measure of her earthly history, with gratitude and expectation.

If, as St. Irenaeus says, she acted the part of an Advocate, a friend in need, even in her mortal life, if as St. Jerome and St. Ambrose say, she was on earth the great pattern of Virgins, if she had a meritorious share in bringing about our redemption, if her maternity was gained by her faith and obedience, if her Divine Son was subject to her, and if she stood by the Cross with a mother's heart and drank in to the full those sufferings which it was her portion to gaze upon, it is impossible that we should not associate these characteristics of her life on earth with her present state of blessedness; and this surely she anticipated, when she said in her hymn that all "generations should call her blessed."

I am aware that, in thus speaking, I am following a line of thought which is rather a meditation than an argument in controversy, and I shall not carry it further; but still, before turning to other topics, it is to the point to inquire, whether the popular astonishment, excited by our belief in the blessed Virgin's present dignity, does not arise from the circumstance that the bulk of men, engaged in matters of this world, have never calmly considered her historical position in the gospels, so as rightly to realize (if I may use the word a second time) what that position imports. I do not claim for the generality of Catholics any greater powers of reflection upon the objects of their faith, than Protestants commonly have; but, putting the run of Catholics aside, there is a sufficient number of religious men among us who, instead of expending their devotional energies (as so many serious Protestants do) on abstract doctrines, such as justification by faith only, or the sufficiency of Holy Scripture, employ themselves in the contemplation of Scripture facts, and bring out before their minds in a tangible form the doctrines involved in them, and give such a substance and color to the sacred history, as to influence their brethren; and their brethren, though superficial themselves, are drawn by their Catholic instinct to accept conclusions which they could not indeed themselves have elicited, but which, when elicited, they feel to be true. However, it would be out of place to pursue this course of reasoning here; and instead of doing so, I shall take what perhaps you may think a very bold step—I shall find the doctrine of our Lady's present exaltation in Scripture.

I mean to find it in the vision of the Woman and Child in the twelfth chapter of the Apocalypse—now here two objections will be made to me at once; first that such an interpretation is but poorly supported by the Fathers, and secondly that in ascribing such a picture of the Madonna (as it may be called) to the Apostolic age, I am committing an anachronism.

As to the former of these objections, I answer as follows: Christians have never gone to Scripture for proof of their doctrines, till there was actual need, from the pressure of controversy—if in those times the Blessed Virgin's dignity was unchallenged on all hands, as a matter of doctrine, Scripture, as far as its argumentative matter was concerned, was likely to remain a sealed book to them. Thus, to take an instance in point; the Catholic party in the Anglican Church (say, the Nonjurors), unable by their theory of religion simply to take their stand on Tradition, and distressed for proof of their doctrines, had their eyes sharpened to scrutinize and to understand in many places the letter of Holy Scripture, which to others brought no instruction. And the peculiarity of their interpretations is this—that these have in themselves great logical cogency, yet are but faintly supported by patristic commentators.

Such is the use of the word *poiein* or *facere* in our Lord's institution of the Holy Eucharist, which, by a reference to the Old Testament, is found to be a word of sacrifice. Such again is *leitourgounton* in the passage in the Acts, "As they ministered to the Lord and fasted," which again is a sacerdotal term. And such the passage in Romans 15:16, in which several terms are used which have an allusion to the sacrificial Eucharistic rite. Such too is St. Paul's repeated message to the household of Onesiphorus, with no mention of Onesiphorus himself, but in one place with the addition of a prayer that "he might find mercy of the Lord" in the day of judgment, which, taking into account its wording and the known usage of the first centuries, we can hardly deny is a prayer for his soul.

Other texts there are, which ought to find a place in ancient controversies, and the omission of which by the Fathers affords matter for more surprise; those for instance, which, according to Middleton's rule, are real proofs of our Lord's divinity, and yet are passed over by Catholic disputants; for these bear upon a then existing controversy of the first moment, and of the most urgent exigency.

As to the second objection which I have supposed, so far from allowing it, I consider that it is built upon a mere imaginary fact, and that the truth of the matter lies in the very contrary direction. The Virgin and Child is not a mere modern idea; on the contrary, it is represented again and again, as every visitor to Rome is aware, in the paintings of the Catacombs. Mary is there drawn with the Divine Infant in her lap, she with hands extended in prayer, He with His hand in the attitude of blessing. No representation can more forcibly convey the doctrine of the high dignity of the Mother, and, I will add, of her influence with her Son.

Why should the memory of His time of subjection be so dear to Christians, and so carefully preserved? The only question to be determined is the precise date of these remarkable monuments of the first age of Christianity. That they belong to the centuries of what Anglicans call the "undivided Church" is certain; but lately investigations have been pursued, which place some of them at an earlier date than any one anticipated as possible.

I am not in a position to quote largely from the works of the Cavaliere de Rossi, who has thrown so much light upon the subject; but I have his *Imagini Scelte*, published in 1863, and they are sufficient for my purpose. In this work he has given us from the Catacombs various representations of the Virgin and Child; the latest of these belong to the early part of the fourth century, but the earliest he believes to be referable to the very age of the apostles. He comes to this conclusion from the style and the skill of its composition, and from the history, locality, and existing inscriptions of the subterranean in which it is found. However, he does not go so far as to insist upon so early a date; yet the utmost concession he makes is to refer the painting to the era of the first Antonines, that is, to a date within half a century of the death of St. John.

I consider then that, as you would use in controversy with Protestants, and fairly, the traditional doctrine of the Church in early times, as an explanation of a particular passage of Scripture, or at least as a suggestion, or as a defense, of the sense which you may wish to put upon it, quite apart from the question whether your interpretation itself is directly traditional, so it is lawful for me, though I have not the positive words of the Fathers on my side, to shelter my own interpretation of the Apostle's vision in the Apocalypse under the fact of the extant pictures of Mother and Child in the Roman Catacombs.

Again, there is another principle of Scripture interpretation which we should hold as well as you, viz., when we speak of a doctrine being contained in Scripture, we do not necessarily mean that it is contained there in direct categorical terms, but that there is no satisfactory way of accounting for the language and expressions of the sacred writers, concerning the subject matter in question, except to suppose that they held concerning it the opinion which we hold—that they would not have spoken as they have spoken, unless they held it. For myself I have ever felt the truth of this principle, as regards the Scripture proof of the Holy Trinity; I should not have found out that doctrine in the sacred text without previous traditional teaching; but, when once it is suggested from without, it commends itself as the one true interpretation, from its appositeness—because no other view of doctrine, which can be ascribed to the inspired writers, so happily solves the obscurities and seeming inconsistencies of their teaching. And now to apply what I have been saying to the passage in the Apocalypse.

If there is an Apostle on whom, à priori, our eyes would be fixed, as likely to teach us about the Blessed Virgin, it is St. John, to whom she was committed by our Lord on the Cross—with whom, as tradition goes, she lived at Ephesus till she was taken away. This anticipation is confirmed à posteriori; for, as I have said above, one of the earliest and fullest of our informants concerning her dignity, as being the second Eve, is Irenaeus, who came to Lyons from Asia Minor, and had been taught by the immediate disciples of St. John. The Apostle's vision is as follows:

> A great sign appeared in heaven: A woman clothed with the Sun, and the Moon under her feet; and on her head a crown of twelve stars. And being with child, she cried travailing in birth, and was in pain to be delivered. And there was seen another sign in heaven; and behold a great red dragon.... And the dragon stood before the woman who was ready to be delivered, that, when she should be delivered, he might devour her son. And she brought forth a man child, who was to rule all nations with an iron rod; and her son was taken up to God and to His throne. And the woman fled into the wilderness.

Now I do not deny, of course, that under the image of the Woman, the Church is signified; but what I would maintain is this, that the Holy Apostle would not have spoken of the Church under this particular image, unless there had existed a blessed Virgin Mary, who was exalted on high, and the object of veneration to all the faithful.

No one doubts that the "man-child" spoken of is an allusion to our Lord: why then is not "the Woman" an allusion to His Mother? This surely is the obvious sense of the words; of course they have a further sense also, which is the scope of the image; doubtless the Child represents the children of the Church, and doubtless the Woman represents the Church; this, I grant, is the real or direct sense, but what is the sense of the symbol under which that real sense is conveyed? Who are the Woman and the Child? I answer, they are not personifications but Persons. This is true of the Child, therefore it is true of the Woman.

But again: not only Mother and Child, but a serpent is introduced into the vision. Such a meeting of man, woman, and serpent has not been found in Scripture since the beginning of Scripture, and now it is found in its end. Moreover, in the passage in the Apocalypse, as if to supply, before Scripture came to an end, what was wanting in its beginning, we are told, and for the first time, that the serpent in Paradise was the evil spirit. If the dragon of St. John is the same as the serpent of [Genesis], and the man-child is "the seed of the woman," why is not the woman herself she, whose seed the man-child is? And, if the first woman is not an allegory, why is the second? If the first woman is Eve, why is not the second Mary?

But this is not all. The image of the woman, according to general Scripture usage, is too bold and prominent for a mere personification. Scripture is not fond of allegories. We have indeed frequent figures there, as when the sacred writers speak of the arm or sword of the Lord; and so too when they speak of Jerusalem or Samaria in the feminine; or of the Church as a bride or as a vine; but they are not much given to dressing up abstract ideas or generalizations in personal attributes. This is the classical rather than the Scriptural style. Xenophon places Hercules between Virtue and Vice, represented as women; Aeschylus introduces into his drama Force and Violence; Virgil gives personality to public rumor or Fame, and Plautus to Poverty.

So on monuments done in the classical style, we see virtues, vices, rivers, renown, death, and the like, turned into human figures of men and women. Certainly I do not deny there are some instances of this method in Scripture, but I say that such poetical compositions are strikingly unlike its usual method. Thus, we at once feel the difference from Scripture, when we betake ourselves to the Pastor of Hermas, and find the Church a woman; to St. Methodius, and find Virtue a woman; and to St. Gregory's poem, and find Virginity again a woman. Scripture deals with types rather than personifications. Israel stands for the chosen people, David for Christ, Jerusalem for heaven.

Consider the remarkable representations, dramatic I may call them, in Jeremiah, Ezechiel, and Hosea: predictions, threatenings, and promises are acted out by those Prophets. Ezechiel is commanded to shave his head, and to divide and scatter his hair; and Ahias [Ahijah] tears his garment, and gives ten out of twelve parts of it to Jeroboam. So too the structure of the imagery in the Apocalypse is not a mere allegorical creation, but is founded on the Jewish ritual.

In like manner our Lord's bodily cures are visible types of the power of His grace upon the soul; and His prophecy of the last day is conveyed under that of the fall of Jerusalem. Even His parables are not simply ideal, but relations of occurrences, which did or might take place, under which was conveyed a spiritual meaning. The description of Wisdom in the Proverbs and other sacred books has brought out the instinct of commentators in this respect. They felt that Wisdom could not be a mere personification, and they determined that it was our Lord: and the later-written of these books, by their own more definite language, warranted that interpretation. Then, when it was found that the Arians used it in derogation of our Lord's divinity, still, unable to tolerate the notion of a mere allegory, commentators applied the description to the Blessed Virgin.

Coming back then to the Apocalyptic vision, I ask, If the Woman ought to be some real person, who can it be whom the Apostle saw, and intends, and delineates, but that same Great Mother to whom the chapters in the Proverbs are accommodated? And let it be observed, moreover, that in this passage, from the allusion made in it to the history of the fall, Mary may be said still to be represented under the character of the Second Eve. I make a farther remark: it is sometimes asked, Why do not the sacred writers mention our Lady's greatness? I answer, she was, or may have been alive, when the Apostles and Evangelists wrote—there was just one book of Scripture certainly written after her death, and that book does (so to say) canonize and crown her.

But if all this be so, if it is really the Blessed Virgin whom Scripture represents as clothed with the sun, crowned with the stars of heaven, and with the moon as her footstool, what height of glory may we not attribute to her? And what are we to say of those who, through ignorance, run counter to the voice of Scripture, to the testimony of the Fathers, to the traditions of East and West, and speak and act contemptuously towards her whom her Lord delighteth to honour?[1]

✠ BIBLIOGRAPHY

Ambrose of Milan. *Exposition of the Holy Gospel According to Saint Luke*. Etna, Calif.: CTOS, 2003.

Aphrahat. *Demonstrations*, vol. 1. Kerala, India: HIRS, 1999.

Aphrahat. *Demonstrations*, vol. 2.. Kerala, India: SEERI, 2005.

Aquilina, Mike. *The Fathers of the Church: An Introduction to the First Christian Teachers*. Huntington, Ind.: Our Sunday Visitor, 2013.

———. *The Mass of the Early Christians*. Huntington, Ind.: Our Sunday Visitor, 2007.

———. *Roots of the Faith: From the Church Fathers to You*. Cincinnati: Servant, 2010.

Bastero, Juan Luis. *Mary, Mother of the Redeemer*. Dublin: Four Courts, 2011.

Bennett, Rod. *Four Witnesses: The Early Church in Her Own Words*. San Francisco: Ignatius, 2002.

Bisconti, Fabrizio, ed. *Temi di Iconografia Paleocristiana*. Vatican City: Pontificio Istituto di Archeologia Cristiana, 2000.

Boss, Sarah Jane, ed. *Mary: The Complete Resource*. New York: Oxford University Press, 2007.

Brightman, F.E. *Liturgies Eastern and Western*. Oxford: Clarendon, 1896.

Brock, Sebastian. *Bride of Light: Hymns on Mary from the Syriac Churches*. Kerala, India: SEERI, 1994.

Brown, Michelle. *In the Beginning: Bibles Before the Year 1000*. Washington, D.C.: Smithsonian, 2007.

Brown, Raymond E. et al, eds., *Mary in the New Testament*. Philadelphia: Fortress, 1978.

Buby, Bertrand. *Mary of Galilee: The Marian Heritage of the Early Church, A Legacy of the First 500 Years*. New York: Alba, 1996.

Bunson, Matthew. *Encyclopedia of Catholic History*. Huntington, Ind.: Our Sunday Visitor, 2004.

Cessario, Romanus. *Perpetual Angelus*. New York: Alba, 1995.

Charlesworth, James H., ed. *The Old Testament Pseudepigrapha: Apocalyptic Literature and Testaments*. New York: Doubleday, 1983.

Crichton, J.D. *Our Lady in the Liturgy*. Collegeville, Minn.: Liturgical, 1997.

Cuming, Geoffrey J. *The Liturgy of St. Mark: Edited from the Manuscripts with a Commentary*. Rome: Pontifical Oriental Institute, 1990.

Daley, Brian J., ed. *On the Dormition of Mary: Early Patristic Homilies*. Crestwood, N.Y.: St. Vladimir's Seminary Press, 1997.

D'Ambrosio, Marcellino. *When the Church Was Young: Voices of the Early Fathers*. Cincinnati: Servant, 2014.

Daniélou, Jean. *Primitive Christian Symbols*. Baltimore: Helicon, 1961.

———. *The Theology of Jewish Christianity*. Chicago: Regnery, 1964.

de Lubac, Henri. *The Motherhood of the Church*. San Francisco: Ignatius, 1982.

———. *The Splendor of the Church*. San Francisco: Ignatius, 1986.

Deiss, Lucien. *Springtime of the Liturgy*. Collegeville, Minn.: Liturgical, 1979.

Deutsch, Bernard F. *Our Lady of Ephesus*. Milwaukee: Bruce, 1965.

du Bourguet, Pierre. *Coptic Art*. London: Methuen, 1971.

———. *Early Christian Art*. New York: William Morrow, 1971.

———. *The Art of the Copts*. New York: Crown, 1967.

Eaton-Krauss, Gabra, Gawdat, and Marianne. *The Treasures of Coptic Art in the Coptic Museum and Churches of Old Cairo*. Cairo: American University in Cairo Press, 2007.

Gambero, Luigi. *Mary and the Fathers of the Church*. San Francisco: Ignatius, 2004.

Louis Ginzberg, *Legends of the Bible*. Philadelphia: Jewish Publication Society, 1992.

Grabar, André. *Christian Iconography: A Study of Its Origins*. Princeton, N.J.: Princeton University Press, 1968.

St. Gregory of Nazianzus. *Selected Orations*. Washington, D.C.: Catholic University of America, 2003.

Haffner, Paul. *The Mystery of Mary*. Chicago: Liturgy Training, 2004.

Hahn, Scott. *Joy to the World*. New York: Image, 2014.

Heider, Andrew B. *The Blessed Virgin Mary in Early Christian Latin Poetry*. Washington, D.C.: Catholic University of America Press, 1918.

Hurtado, Larry W. *The Earliest Christian Artifacts: Manuscripts and Christian Origins*. Grand Rapids: Eerdmans, 2006.

James, M.R. *The New Testament Apocrypha*. Berkeley, Calif.: Apocryphile, 2004.

Jensen, Robin Margaret. *Understanding Early Christian Art*. London: Routledge, 2000.

St. Jerome. *St. Jerome's Commentaries on Galatians, Titus, and Philemon*. Notre Dame, Ind.: University of Notre Dame Press, 2010.

Jungmann, Joseph. *The Mass of the Roman Rite: Its Origins and Development*. Two volumes. New York: Benziger, 1951.

———. *The Place of Christ in Liturgical Prayer*. Collegeville, Minn.: Liturgical, 1989.

Kaniyamparampil, Emmanuel. *The Spirit of Life: A Study of the Holy Spirit in the Early Syriac Tradition*. Kerala, India: Oriental Institute of Religious Studies India, 2003.

Koester, Helmut. *Introduction to the New Testament*. Vol. 2, *History and Literature of Early Christianity*. Philadelphia: Fortress, 1982.

Lawrence of Brindisi. *The Mariale*. Delhi, India: Media House, 2007.

Lienhard, Joseph T. *St. Joseph in Early Christianity: Devotion and Theology*. Philadelphia: St. Joseph's University Press, 1999.

Lowden, John. *Early Christian and Byzantine Art*. London: Phaidon, 1997.

Luijendijk, AnneMarie. *Forbidden Oracles? The Gospel of the Lots of Mary*. Tubingen, Germany: Mohr Siebeck, 2014.

———. *Greetings in the Lord: Early Christians and the Oxyrhynchus Papyri*. Cambridge, Mass.: Harvard, 2008.

Marucchi, Orazio. *Manual of Christian Archeology*. Paterson, N.J.: St. Anthony Guild, 1949.

Maunder, Chris, ed. *The Origins of the Cult of the Virgin Mary*. London: Burns and Oates, 2008.

Maximus the Confessor. *The Life of the Virgin*. New Haven, Conn.: Yale, 2012.

McDonnell, Kilian. *The Baptism of Jesus in the Jordan: The Trinitarian and Cosmic Order of Salvation*. Collegeville, Minn.: Michael Glazier, 1997.

McGuckin, John. *Saint Cyril of Alexandria and the Christological Controversy*. Crestwood, N.Y.: St. Vladimir's Seminary Press, 2004.

Meinardus, Otto F.A. *Two Thousand Years of Coptic Christianity*. Cairo: American University in Cairo, 1999.

Meyer, Marvin, and Richard Smith, eds. *Ancient Christian Magic: Coptic Texts of Ritual Power*. San Francisco: Harper, 1994.

Murray, Robert. *Symbols of Church and Kingdom: A Study in Early Syriac Tradition*. Piscataway, N.J.: Gorgias, 1975.

Newman, John Henry. *The Church of the Fathers*. Notre Dame, Ind.: Notre Dame University Press, 2002.

———. *Essay on the Development of Christian Doctrine*. London: Longmans, Green, 1909.

———. *The Mystical Rose*. New York: Scepter, 1996.

O'Carroll, Michael. *Theotokos: A Theological Encyclopedia of the Blessed Virgin Mary*. Eugene, Oreg.: Wipf and Stock, 2000.

Papandrea, James L. *Reading the Early Church Fathers: From the Didache to Nicaea*. New York: Paulist, 2012.

Pearson, Birger A., and James E. Goehring, eds. *The Roots of Egyptian Christianity*. Philadelphia: Fortress, 1986.

Pelikan, Jaroslav. *Mary Through the Centuries: Her Place in the History of Culture*. New Haven, Conn.: Yale, 1996.

Plumpe, Joseph C. *Mater Ecclesia: An Inquiry into the Concept of the Church as Mother in Early Christianity*. Washington, D.C.: Catholic University of America Press, 1943.

Rahner, Hugo. *Our Lady and the Church*. Bethesda, Md.: Zaccheus, 2004.

Reynolds, Brian K. *Gateway to Heaven: Marian Doctrine and Devotion, Image and Typology in the Patristic and Medieval Periods*. Hyde Park, N.Y.: New City, 2012.

Scheeben, M.J. *Mariology*. London: B. Herder, 1946.

Shoemaker, Stephen J. *Ancient Traditions of the Virgin Mary's Dormition and Assumption*. Oxford: Oxford University Press, 2002.

Sommer, Carl J. *We Look for a Kingdom: The Everyday Lives of the Early Christians*. San Francisco: Ignatius, 2007.

Spier, Jeffrey, et al. *Picturing the Bible: The Earliest Christian Art*. New Haven, Conn.: Yale University Press, 2009.

Stark, Rodney. *The Rise of Christianity: How the Obscure Jesus Movement Became the Dominant Religious Force in the Western World in a Few Centuries*. San Francisco: HarperCollins, 1997.

Tanner, Norman P. *Decrees of the Ecumenical Councils*, vol. 1. London: Sheed and Ward, 1992.

Thurian, Max. *Mary: Mother of All Christians*. New York: Herder and Herder, 1964.

Tixeront, Joseph. *History of Dogmas*. Westminster, Md.: Christian Classics, 1984.

Walsh, John Evangelist. *The Bones of St. Peter*. Manila: Sinag-Tala, 1987.

Weinandy, Thomas G., and Daniel A. Keating. *The Theology of St. Cyril of Alexandria: A Critical Appreciation*. London: T&T Clark, 2003.

Weitzmann, Kurt. *Late Antique and Early Christian Book Illumination*. New York: George Braziller, 1977.

Whitehead, Kenneth. *One, Holy, Catholic, and Apostolic: The Early Church Was the Catholic Church*. San Francisco: Ignatius, 2000.

Wilken, Robert Louis. *The First Thousand Years*. New Haven, Conn.: Yale University, 2012.

Yarnold, Edward. *The Awe-Inspiring Rites of Initiation*. Collegeville, Minn.: Liturgical, 1994.

Zuzic, Marko. *A Short History of St. John in Ephesus*. Lima, Ohio: American Society of Ephesus, 1960.

✥ NOTES

DEDICATION

1. St. Ambrose of Milan, *Letters*, 63.

ACKNOWLEDGMENTS

1. Philip Schaff, ed., *The Ante-Nicene Fathers* and *The Nicene and Post-Nicene Fathers*.

CHAPTER ONE

1. Stephen J. Shoemaker, *Ancient Traditions of the Virgin Mary's Dormition and Assumption* (Oxford: Oxford University Press, 2002), pp. 288–289.
2. St. Basil the Great, *Letters* 223.3, 5.
3. Tertullian, trans. S. Thelwall, *On the Veiling of Virgins*, chap. 1, in *Fathers of the Third Century*, vol. 4, *Ante-Nicene Fathers*, Christian Classics Ethereal Library, www.ccel.org.
4. St. Irenaeus of Lyons, *Against Heresies*, bk. 3, chap. 24, no. 1, in *The Apostolic Fathers with Justin Martyr and Irenaeus*, vol. 1, *Ante-Nicene Fathers*, Christian Classics Ethereal Library.
5. St. Augustine, *City of God*, 16.2.
6. St. Cyril of Alexandria, *Letter to John of Antioch about Peace*.
7. See Geoffrey J. Cuming, ed., *The Liturgy of St. Mark* (Rome: Pontificium Institutum Studiorum Orientalium, 1990), p. 29.
8. Archeologists have recently recovered a papyrus in Egypt that includes this prayer to the Mother of God, the *Sub Tuum*, which is still in use today. We say more about it in chapter seven.
9. See St. Gregory of Nazianzus, *Orations* 24.11.
10. Anonymous, *The Sibylline Oracles*, 8.474–475. "For he to erring men / Gave, in seven ages for repentance, signs / By the hands of a virgin undefiled.

11. Origen, *Commentary on John* 1.6.
12. St. Ambrose of Milan, *Commentary on Luke* 7.5.

Chapter Two

1. Tertullian, *Five Books Against Marcion*, 4.5.
2. See Origen, *Homilies on Luke*, trans. Joseph T. Lienhard (Washington, D.C.: Catholic University of America Press, 1996), 6.7, p. 26.
3. St. Ambrose of Milan, *On the Mysteries* 9.59; *On the Sacraments* 4.17.
4. St. Ambrose of Milan, *Exposition of the Gospel of Luke* 2.8.
5. Origen, trans. Joseph Lienhard, *Homilies on Luke*, 9.1–2, pp. 37–38.
6. St. Jerome, *Homilies on John* 1.1.
7. See, for example, Aphrahat, *Demonstrations* 14.33.
8. St. Hilary of Poitiers, *Tractate on the Psalms* 118.12.
9. See, for example, Origen, *Homilies on Luke* 20.5.
10. See Kilian McDonnell, O.S.B., *The Baptism of Jesus in the Jordan: The Trinitarian and Cosmic Order of Salvation* (Collegeville, Minn.: Liturgical, 1996), p. 74.
11. See St. Ephrem, *Hymns on the Church* 49.7.
12. St. Augustine of Hippo, *Harmony of the Gospels* 4.10.11.
13. St. Hilary of Poitiers, *On the Councils* 27.70.
14. For a full study of the Fathers' treatment of St. Joseph, see Joseph T. Lienhard, S.J., *St. Joseph in Early Christianity: Devotion and Theology* (Philadelphia: St. Joseph's University Press, 1999).
15. See St. Gregory of Nyssa, *On the Birth of Christ*.
16. See Appendix, John Henry Newman, "The Dignity of Mary."

Chapter Three

1. See Tertullian, *On Baptism* 17.
2. Quoted in Eusebius, *Church History* 6.12.2.
3. On the dating of *The Ascension of Isaiah*, see Torleif Elgvin, "Jewish Christian Editing of the Old Testament Pseudepigrapha,"

in Oskar Skarsaune, *Jewish Believers in Jesus: The Early Centuries* (Peabody, Mass.: Hendrickson, 2007), pp. 292–295. See also Richard Bauckham, *The Fate of the Dead: Studies on the Jewish and Christian Apocalypses* (Leiden, England: Brill, 1998), pp. 363–390, and Jean Daniélou, *The Theology of Jewish Christianity* (Chicago: Regnery, 1964), pp. 12–13.

4. *The Ascension of Isaiah* 11:2–15, EarlyChristianWritings.com.

5. Dating of the *Odes* is difficult. The fourth *Ode* seems to refer to the Jewish temple in Leontopolis, Egypt, as if it were still standing. The Leontopolis temple was destroyed in A.D. 70 or shortly thereafter. J.H. Charlesworth writes that "a date long after 100 is unlikely." See his "Odes of Solomon" in David Noel Freedman, ed., *Anchor Bible Dictionary*, vol. 6 (New Haven, Conn.: Yale, 1992), p. 114. For a still earlier dating, see P. Smith, "The Disciples of John and the Odes of Solomon," in *The Monist*, April 1915, pp. 161–199.

6. Anonymous, *Odes of Solomon,* Ode 19, verses 6–10, in Rutherford H. Platt, *The Forgotten Books of Eden* (New York: Alpha House, 1926), p. 116.

7. *Odes of Solomon* 33.5–7, adapted from Platt, p. 132.

8. See the discussion of intercession in J.L. Lightfoot, trans. and ed., *The Sibylline Oracles* (Oxford: Oxford University Press, 2007), pp. 434, 518, 520, 527.

9. Lightfoot, pp. 608–640.

10. See St. Justin Martyr, *First Apology* 46.1–4, earlyChristian writings.com.

11. St. Ignatius of Antioch, *Letter to the Ephesians* 19:1.

12. St. Ignatius of Antioch, *Letter to the Ephesians* 19:2–3.

13. St. Hippolytus of Rome, *On the Blessings of Isaac and Jacob* 2.

14. St. Justin Martyr, *Dialogue with Trypho* 78; see also 70.

15. See Origen, *Against Celsus* 1.51.

Chapter Four

1. Data on baby names is stored by the U.S. Social Security administration and available on its website: http://www.ssa.gov.

2. AnneMarie Luijendijk, *Greetings in the Lord: Early Christians and the Oxyrhynchus Papyri* (Cambridge, Mass.: Harvard, 2008), p. 48.

3. See Ralph Waldo Emerson, *Essays: Second Series.*

4. Plato, *Cratylus* 439 and 430.

5. St. Jerome, *On the Interpretation of Hebrew Names.*

6. Philo, *On Husbandry* 17.80–81.

7. *Infancy James* 7.

8. St. Ephrem of Syria, *Hymns on the Nativity* 25.14.

9. See Larry W. Hurtado, *The Earliest Christian Artifacts: Manuscripts and Christian Origins* (Grand Rapids, Mich.: Eerdmans, 2006), pp. 96, 134.

10. See Getatcheu Haile, *Catalogue of the Ethiopic Manuscript Imaging Project* (Eugene, Oreg.: Wipf & Stock, 2009), p. 37.

11. See the discussion of the Nazareth excavations at christusrex.org/www1/ofm/san/TSnzarc2.html (retrieved May 13, 2015).

12. See the discussion of Marian graffiti in John Evangelist Walsh, *The Bones of St. Peter* (Manila: Sinag-Tala, 1987), pp. 97–99.

13. Anonymous, *Carmen adversus Marcionem*, 179.

14. St. Ambrose of Milan, *On the Death of Theodosius*, 44.

CHAPTER FIVE

1. Peter Schäfer, *Jesus in the Talmud* (Princeton, N.J.: Princeton University Press, 2007), p. 2.

2. Schäfer, p. 10.

3. Schäfer, p. 2.

4. R. Joseph Hoffmann, trans. and ed., *Celsus: On the True Doctrine* (New York: Oxford University Press, 1987), p. 57.

5. Quoted in Origen, *Against Celsus* 1.39.

6. St. Justin Martyr, *Dialogue with Trypho* 43.8 and 67.1

7. St. Cyril of Jerusalem, *Catechetical Lectures* 12.

8. St. Irenaeus of Lyons, *Against Heresies* 1.10.1.

9. Tertullian, *On the Veiling of Virgins* 1.

10. Aristides, *Apology* 2.

11. St. Clement of Rome, *Letter to the Corinthians* 38.2.

12. St. Ignatius of Antioch, *Letter to Polycarp* 5.
13. Quoted in Richard Walzer, *Galen on Jews and Christians* (London: Oxford, 1949), p. 65.
14. St. Athenagoras of Athens, *Plea for the Christians* 33.
15. St. Ambrose of Milan, *Concerning Virginity* bk. 2, chap. 2, no. 6.
16. St. Gregory of Nyssa, *On the Birth of Christ*, quoted in Luigi Gambero, *Mary and the Fathers of the Church: The Blessed Virgin Mary in Patristic Thought* (San Francisco: Ignatius, 1999), p. 157.
17. St. Jerome, *Homilies* 87.
18. St. Basil the Great, *On the Holy Generation of Christ* 5.
19. Tertullian, *On the Flesh of Christ* 23.
20. St. Jerome, *Against Helvidius* 6.
21. St. Jerome, *Against Helvidius* 4.

CHAPTER SIX
1. St. Justin Martyr, *Dialogue with Trypho*, chap. 100.
2. St. Irenaeus of Lyons, *Against Heresies* 5.21.1.
3. For example, in *Against Heresies* 3.18.7, 3.22.4, and 5.19.1.
4. St. Irenaeus of Lyons, *Against Heresies* 4.33.11.
5. St. Irenaeus of Lyons, *Against Heresies* 4.33.4.
6. St. Irenaeus of Lyons, *Against Heresies* 3.22.4. Pope Francis has been one of the chief promoters of "Our Lady Undoer of Knots." When Fr. Jorge Mario Bergoglio was studying in Germany, he was stunned by a Bavarian painting of *Holy Mary, Our Lady Untier of Knots*. He acquired a copy, brought it to Argentina, and promoted devotion to Mary under this title. Since his ascension to the Chair of Peter, the devotion has gained popularity throughout the world.
7. Tertullian, *On the Flesh of Christ* 17.
8. Tertullian, *On the Veiling of Virgins* 5.
9. Jerome, *Letters* 22.21.
10. Prudentius, *Hymn Before Meat*.
11. St. Epiphanius, *Panarion* 78.11.
12. St. Epiphanius, *Panarion* 78.17, quoted in Gambero, pp. 128–129.

13. See the discussion in Henri de Lubac, *The Splendor of the Church* (San Francisco: Ignatius, 1986), pp. 318–319.

14. St. Ambrose of Milan, *Exposition of the Gospel of Luke* 2.7.

15. See examples in Gambero, p. 115.

16. See Joseph C. Plumpe, *Mater Ecclesia: An Inquiry into the Concept of the Church as Mother in Early Christianity* (Washington, D.C.: Catholic University of America Press, 1943).

17. See Robin Margaret Jensen, *Understanding Early Christian Art* (London: Routledge, 2000), p. 180. See also John Lowden, *Early Christian and Byzantine* Art (London: Phaidon, 1997), pp. 48–49.

CHAPTER SEVEN

1. A well-told and entertaining account of the council can be found in John McGuckin, *Saint Cyril of Alexandria and the Christological Controversy* (Crestwood, N.Y.: St. Vladimir's Seminary Press, 2004).

2. Letter of Cyril of Alexandria to Nestorius, included in the acts of the Council of Ephesus.

3. In its most ancient form, the opening phrases of the *Sub Tuum* may be rendered from the Greek as "Under the protection of your heart (or womb), we take refuge." Later spiritual writers, especially in the French school represented by St. John Eudes, would employ this intuition in devotion to Mary's Immaculate Heart and consideration of her role as Mother of the Church.

4. St. Alexander of Alexandria, *Letters on Arianism* 1.12.

5. *Oration of Constantine* 11.

6. St. Athanasius, *Against the Arians* 3.29.

7. Prudentius, *Hymn on the Divinity of Christ,* pp. 435–436.

8. St. Gregory of Nazianzus, *Letters* 101.

9. Pseudo-Ignatius, *Letter to John the Holy Presbyter.*

10. Julian the Apostate, *Against the Galilaeans,* bk. 1, excerpted from Cyril of Alexandria, *Contra Julianum,* pp. 319–433, www.tertullian.org.

11. Pope John Paul II and Mar Dinkha IV, *Common Christological Declaration Between the Catholic Church and the Assyrian Church of the East*, November 11, 1994, www.vatican.va.

CHAPTER EIGHT

1. St. Athanasius or Pseudo-Athanasius, *On Virginity*, quoted in Gambero, p. 101.
2. St. Ephrem of Syria, *Nisibene Hymns* 27.8.
3. St. Ambrose of Milan, *Commentary on Psalm 118* [119] 22, 30.
4. St. Hippolytus of Rome, *Fragment on Psalm 22 or 23*.
5. St. Augustine of Hippo, *On Nature and Grace 36*.
6. St. Ephrem of Syria, *Hymns on the Nativity* 11.
7. St. Ambrose, Exposition of Luke 10.42, quoted in Michael O'Carroll, *Theotokos: A Theological Encyclopedia of the Blessed Virgin Mary* (Eugene, Oreg.: Wipf and Stock, 1982), p. 19.
8. St. Gregory of Nazianzus, *Orations* 38.13.
9. See *Catechism of the Catholic Church*, 493.
10. St. Augustine of Hippo, *On Nature and Grace 42*.
11. See Ephrem of Syria, *Hymns on the Church* 36.3–6.
12. St. Ambrose of Milan, *On Virginity* 2.2.7.
13. St. Augustine of Hippo, *The Christian Combat*, chap. 22 (24).
14. Hymn 26, verse 8, in Sebastian Brock, *Bride of Light: Hymns on Mary from the Syriac Churches* (Kerala, India: SEERI, 1994), p. 90.
15. Ephrem, *Precationes ad Deiparam* 3, adapted from Thomas Livius, *The Blessed Virgin in the Fathers of the First Six Centuries* (London: Burns and Oates, 1893), p. 213.

CHAPTER NINE

1. Pope Pius XII, *Munificentissimus Deus*, 44, www.vatican.va.
2. Pope Pius XII, *Munificentissimus Deus*, 5.
3. Reinhold Niebuhr, "The Increasing Isolation of the Catholic Church," *Christianity and Crisis*, September 18, 1950, 113–114.

The essay also appears in his collection *Essays in Applied Christianity* (New York: Meridian, 1959), pp. 244–246.

4. Tillich, Paul. *A History of Christian Thought: From Its Judaic and Hellenistic Origins to Existentialism* (New York: Simon and Schuster, 1972), p. 224.

5. As quoted in David Scott, "In Her End, the Promise of Our Beginning," originally published in *Our Sunday Visitor*, August 15, 2004, and archived at davidscottwritings.com.

6. Richard Bauckham, *The Fate of the Dead: Studies on Jewish and Christian Apocalypses* (Leiden: Brill, 1998), pp. 358–360.

7. Stephen J. Shoemaker, *Ancient Traditions of the Virgin Mary's Dormition and Assumption* (Oxford: Oxford University, 2002).

8. Stephen J. Shoemaker, "The Ancient Dormition Apocrypha and the Origins of Marian Piety: Early Evidence of Marian Intercession from Late Ancient Palestine," 2011, archived at Academia.edu.

9. Epiphanius, *Panarion* 78.23.

10. Epiphanius, *Panarion* 79.5, quoted in Shoemaker, "The Ancient Dormition Apocrypha."

11. A third figure assumed into heaven is actually the first to appear in the biblical canon: Enoch. His story in the book of Genesis is cryptic: "Enoch walked with God; and he was not, for God took him" (Genesis 5:24). The book of Sirach elaborates slightly: "Enoch pleased the Lord, and was taken up" (44:16; see also 49:14). The Letter to the Hebrews (11:5) adds further details: "By faith Enoch was taken up so that he should not see death; and he was not found, because God had taken him." Enoch does not, as far as we know, figure in the early Fathers' discussion of Mary.

12. St. Ephrem of Syria, *Hymns on the Nativity* 8.

13. Anonymous, Hymn 29, verse 1, in Brock, p. 99.

14. Simon the Potter, Hymn 3, verse 3, in Brock, p. 104.

15. St. Ephrem of Syria, *Hymns on the Nativity* 9.

16. St. Ephrem of Syria, *Hymns on the Nativity* 1:35f.

17. Shoemaker, *Ancient Traditions*, pp. 378–379.

CHAPTER TEN

1. Pope Blessed Paul VI called upon Mary as "Star of the evangelization ever renewed which the Church, docile to her Lord's command, must promote and accomplish, especially in these times which are difficult but full of hope!" (*Evangelii Nuntiandi*, Evangelization in the Modern World, December 8, 1975, no. 82). Pope St. John Paul II used the title "Star of Evangelization" for several years before adding the penultimate word *New*. See Pope John Paul II, *Novo Millennio Ineunte*, no. 58; Pope Benedict XVI, Homily at Mass for the Opening of the Synod of Bishops, October 7, 2012; and Pope Francis, *Evangelii Gaudium*, 288. See also Cardinal Donald Wuerl, *Relatio Post Disceptationem*, Synod of Bishops, October 17, 2012, www.vatican.va.

2. St. Cyril of Alexandria, *Homilies* 4.

3. See the sociological analysis of Rodney Stark, *The Rise of Christianity: How the Obscure Jesus Movement Became the Dominant Religious Force in the Western World in a Few Centuries* (San Francisco: HarperCollins, 1997). He supplements the study in his book *Cities of God: The Real Story of How Christianity Became an Urban Movement and Conquered Rome* (San Francisco: Harper, 2007).

4. See Appendix.

5. See Gregory of Nyssa, *Life of Gregory the Wonderworker*.

6. For a fascinating discussion of this text, see A. Suciu, "'Me, This Wretched Sinner': A Coptic Fragment from the Vision of Theophilus Concerning the Flight of the Holy Family to Egypt," *Vigiliae Christianae* 67 (2013), pp. 436–450.

7. St. Gregory the Great, *Dialogues* 17; see also 12.

CHAPTER ELEVEN

1. See Kurt Weitzmann, *Late Antique and Early Christian Book Illumination* (New York: George Braziller, 1977), pp. 97–98; Michelle Brown, *In the Beginning: Bibles Before the Year 1000* (Washington, D.C.: Smithsonian, 2007), p. 300.

2. See AnneMarie Luijendijk, *Forbidden Oracles? The Gospel of the Lots of Mary* (Tubingen: Mohr Siebeck, 2014).

3. See Marvin Meyer and Richard Smith, eds., *Ancient Christian Magic: Coptic Texts of Ritual Power* (San Francisco: Harper, 1994), pp. 131, 283.

4. Andrew B. Heider, S.M., *The Blessed Virgin Mary in Early Christian Latin Poetry* (Washington, D.C.: Catholic University of America Press, 1918), p. 7.

5. It is a central point of his book *On Holy Images.*

6. St. Athanasius or Pseudo-Athanasius, quoted in Gambero, p. 101.

7. St. Athanasius or Pseudo-Athanasius, quoted in Gambero, p. 106.

8. St. Amphilochius, quoted in Gambero, p. 170.

9. St. Irenaeus of Lyons, *Against Heresies* 3.22.4.

10. St. Athanasius, *Letters* 60.4 and 61.3.

11. St. Jerome, *Letters* 22.41.

APPENDIX

1. Cardinal John Henry Newman, *Certain Difficulties Felt by Anglicans in Catholic Teaching Considered* (London: Longmans, Green, 1900), pp. 50–61, www.newmanreader.org.

ABOUT THE AUTHORS

Mike Aquilina is the author of more than forty books, including *Yours Is the Church, Roots of the Faith,* and *Good Pope, Bad Pope.* He has hosted nine series on EWTN and two documentary films on the saints of the early Church.

Fr. Frederick W. Gruber is a priest of the Diocese of Pittsburgh, serving in a parish and as a high-school chaplain. He pursued graduate studies at the Marianum, Rome's Pontifical institute for the study of Mariology.